Philosophy for Militants

Philosophy
for Militants

ALAIN BADIOU

Translated with a foreword by Bruno Bosteels

VERSO
London • New York

This paperback edition first published by Verso 2015
First published in the English language 2012
Translation and foreword © Bruno Bosteels 2012, 2015
First published as *La relation énigmatique entre philosophie et politique*
© Germina 2011

1 3 5 7 9 10 8 6 4 2

Verso
UK: 6 Meard Street, London W1F 0EG
US: 388 Atlantic Ave, Brooklyn, NY 11217
www.versobooks.com

Verso is the imprint of New Left Books

ISBN-13: 978-1-78168-869-4 (PB)
eISBN-13: 978-1-84467-987-4 (US)
eISBN-13: 978 1-78168-448-1 (UK)

British Library Cataloguing in Publication Data
A catalogue record for this book is available from the British Library

Library of Congress Cataloging-in-Publication Data
A catalog record for this book is available from the Library of Congress

Typeset in Bodoni Book by Hewer UK Ltd, Edinburgh
Printed in the United States

Contents

Translator's Foreword

1

What better way to preface this charming set of talks on the relationship between politics and philosophy than by asking to what extent they meet the challenge of providing a 'philosophy for militants', as the title of the English translation would indicate?[1] In fact, being a clever marketing ploy on the part of the publisher, this title at first did not sit well with the author – even though he also confessed that he could not come up with a more appropriate one either. This is because Alain Badiou's entire oeuvre can be said to lead to the conclusion that philosophy cannot, or should not, provide political activists and militants with an answer to that classical question: What is to be done?

Regardless of whether Lenin had this view in mind when he famously borrowed the phrasing of that question from Nikolai Chernyshevsky, there certainly exists a common view according to which the task of the philosopher as an

---

1   In the original French edition this collection carries a much simpler and safer title, *La relation énigmatique entre philosophie et politique* – that is, the same title as the one used for the first talk: 'The Enigmatic Relationship between Philosophy and Politics'.

intellectual would consist in telling the masses what is to be done. Even Badiou himself, in the preface to his *Theory of the Subject* published forty years ago, may seem to have been seduced by this self-serving image of the philosopher, insofar as he quotes the people on the barricades during the Paris Commune, in the words of Julien Gracq, as crying out for orders that presumably ought to be forthcoming from the intellectuals: 'Where are the orders? Where is the plan?'[2] For Badiou, whose thinking at this stage is still sutured onto politics under the influence of a strongly Maoist-inflected Marxism, the most unbearable of nightmares would be to be exposed to such a figure of the intellectual who 'wanders around like a lost dog from one barricade to the other, unable to do anything at all', except 'distributing in disorderly fashion vouchers for herrings, bullets, and fire' to the rebellious masses – a nightmarish image that can be avoided, still according to Badiou, only by inventing a creative new linkage between philosophers and militants as part of an even more encompassing overhaul of the relation between intellectuals and workers: 'It is clear to me that to ward off this risk supposes a thorough reshuffling that certainly touches upon the intellectuals but also upon the workers, for what is at stake is the advent between them of an unheard of type of vicinity, of a previously unthinkable political topology.'[3] In fact, part of this new vicinity or topology will involve a

---

2   See Alain Badiou, *Theory of the Subject*, trans. and introduced by Bruno Bosteels (London: Continuum, 2009), p. xlii.
3   Ibid.

growing awareness of the fact that philosophy cannot and should not be programmatic in the classical sense of providing workers and militants with orders for what is to be done.

Already in the context of his next major work, *Being and Event*, Badiou shows much more reluctance before becoming prescriptive in that older sense. In this regard, an interesting but little-known piece of anecdotal evidence is worth developing in some detail. Indeed, when, as part of his investigations for *Being and Event*, Badiou took up the question of deciding whether the factory still represented a strategic site for political struggles today, and thus whether the traditional Marxist paradigm for thinking of politics could still be applicable, his conclusion on the one hand seemed to be resoundingly affirmative, even to the point of becoming openly prescriptive. Thus, Badiou first attempts to define the essence of Marxism: 'Reduced to its bare bones, Marxism is jointly the hypothesis of a politics of non-domination – a politics subtracted from the count of the State – and the designation of the most significant event sites of modernity, those whose singularity is maximal, which are worker sites.' The strength of the classical Marxist paradigm, in other words, would be both political and analytical. In fact, the difficulty consists precisely in coming to terms with the fact that the analytical element is conditioned by the retroactive effect of actual political interventions – without allowing the latter to be derived directly or necessarily from the former. Badiou also writes:

Now, I maintain that this is what Marx was the first to perceive, at a time when factories were in fact seldom counted in the general historical presentation. The vast analytic constructions of *Capital* are the retroactive foundation of what for him was a pre-predicative evidence: that modern politics could not be formulated, even as a hypothesis, otherwise than by proposing an interpretation-in-subject of these astounding hysterias of the social in which workers named the hidden void of the capitalist situation, by naming their own unpresentation.

This insight into the double gesture of Marxism as both analytic construction and political intervention, finally, explains why Badiou, even in the context of *Being and Event*, can appear to remain prescriptive by concluding that the hypothesis of an emancipatory politics today must continue to anchor itself in the reference to the workers in the factory as a key site – if not the only one – of all possible political events: 'That is the reason why it remains legitimate to call oneself a Marxist, if one maintains that politics is possible.'[4]

On the other hand, however, Badiou in the end decided not to publish these reflections as part of *Being and Event*. Instead, he reserved them exclusively for *Le Perroquet*, which was the newsletter of his political organisation at the time. In part, his reasons for doing so were simply logistical. Indeed,

---

4   Alain Badiou, 'L'usine comme site événementiel', *Le Perroquet: Quinzomadaire d'opinion* 62/63 (April–May 1986), p. 6. Translated into English as 'The Factory as Event Site', trans. Alberto Toscano and Nina Power, *Prelom* 8 (1991), p. 176 (translation modified).

Badiou had originally foreseen many more meditations than the thirty-seven that now make up *Being and Event* – with exemplifying illustrations for each of the four conditions of philosophy, which are politics, art, science and love. This turned out to be physically and conceptually unmanageable. But, all logistics aside, there was also an important methodological reason for omitting the few pages of 'The Factory as Event Site' from the vast philosophical system that is *Being and Event*. That is to say, as Badiou himself explains in an introductory note written for *Le Perroquet*, by excluding those pages he is also trying to avoid the traditional role of philosophy as the mother of all discourses, capable of setting the agenda for politics. 'I have withdrawn them, together with others', writes Badiou about the pages in question, 'in order to avoid any false perceptions of the kind: politics is the daughter to philosophy. Because it is the opposite that is true. Philosophy – as Hegel but already Plato knew full well – stands under the condition of procedures of thought that are external to it, among which we find, at the very least, science, art and politics.'[5]

For Badiou, in other words, philosophy cannot and should not play any hegemonic role over politics, for the simple reason that it is rather philosophy which is always conditioned, whether knowingly or not, by actually existing forms of politics, science and so on. More broadly speaking, philosophy is incapable of producing any events or truths of

---

5   Badiou, 'L'usine comme site événementiel', p. 1. This explanatory note is not included in the English translation.

its own, be they political or otherwise. Instead, philosophy is conditioned by events that are not its own making. This also means, incidentally, that all the talk about 'the Badiou event' in philosophy, and about the 'fidelity' of certain commentators to this event, is purely nonsensical. Such talk is strictly incompatible with one of the basic principles behind Badiou's own philosophy, according to which events happen only in other, nonphilosophical domains such as art or politics, the primacy of which constitutes a fundamental premise behind the materialist orientation of this philosophy, as opposed to the typically idealist orientation of philosophies bent upon engendering their truth content out of the activity of the pure concept.

2

However, 'Philosophy for Militants', while clearly running counter to certain basic assumptions behind Badiou's philosophy, is not a complete misnomer either. To this day, indeed, Badiou has never given up on the idea that philosophy can and must be at the service, if not of the people, as he would have said during his Maoist years, then at least of the few practical truths of which human beings occasionally are capable. 'A philosophy worthy of the name – that which begins with Parmenides – is in any case antinomical to the service of goods, inasmuch as it endeavours to be at the service of truths, because it is always possible to endeavour to be at the service of something that one does not constitute oneself', Badiou postulates in *Being and Event*, once more confirming the primacy of practical truths over philosophy, but now adding the useful subservience of philosophy to such truths: 'Philosophy is thus at the service of art, of science and of politics. Whether it is also capable of being at the service of love is more doubtful (art, on the other hand, as a mixed procedure, supports the truths of love).'[6]

So, unable to produce any truths of its own, philosophy must be able to be at the service of politics and other thought-practices, such as art or science, without for this reason becoming hegemonic over them. What then is the precise nature of this enigmatic relation between politics and philosophy? How exactly can philosophy be at the service of politics without telling militants what is to be done?

Roughly speaking, we can distinguish four basic figures in the articulation between philosophy and politics:

1. Especially in the Marxist view, this articulation ideally takes the form of the unity, or fusion, between theory and practice. Philosophy thus would set up a future ideal to which reality must adjust itself, or which strives to realise itself in actual historical practice. We can call this first articulation a figure of prescriptive realisation or normative application.

2. Based on the primacy of practice, philosophy can also see its role as raising actually existing practices to the dignity of the concept. In this case, the articulation

---

6   Alain Badiou, *Being and* Event, trans. Oliver Feltham (London: Continuum, 2005), p. 341 (translation modified).

adopts the figure of a speculative reflection, whereby philosophy always risks losing its materialist credentials in favour of its inherent idealist temptation.

3. Political philosophy, without needing to give in to the pressures of history, can also in all tranquility lay claim to its status as a science, if not more banally as a discipline or department within the contest of faculties of the modern university, the principal occupation of which is then the comparative evaluation of the uses and advantages of various regimes of power: democracy and aristocracy, plutocracy and anarchy, absolutism and republicanism, and so on. Not only does the plurality of regimes that are thus evaluated give the discipline of political philosophy a vaguely democratic appeal, but also the historical insufficiency – no regime being able to match its ideal constitution – opens the prospect of a minimal historicisation of past instantiations of the political, leading up to democracy as the least bad of all possible political regimes. In the famous words of Winston Churchill: 'Democracy is the worst form of government except for all those others that have been tried.'

4. In addition to the figures of realisation, reflection and evaluation, political philosophers over the past few decades have also attempted to inject a tragic element into their field by insisting on the essential unthinkability of the political as such. Whether this pathos of the impossibility of thinking politics is said to be due to the inability of the concept ever to cover its content

without residue or remainder, or else is ascribed to the antagonistic essence of politics as struggle which resists being subsumed under a stable norm, the fact is that many contemporary thinkers see a certain antinomy, or paradox, as the fundamental feature of the articulation between philosophy and politics – with the latter typically being redefined in terms of a certain unpolitical, or impolitical, core. Shipwrecked on the cliffs of political antagonism, the concept of the political now restored to its unpolitical core thus surreptitiously acquires the aura of being the only figure in which philosophy can still claim to be equivalent to a revolution in the era of the historical collapse or failure of the ideal of the historico-political revolution itself. Ostensibly giving up on its traditional hegemonic role, political philosophy nonetheless continues to attribute to itself a radicalism without which all really existing political experiments risk ignoring the antinomies that lie dormant within them.

When Badiou proposes to raise anew the age-old question about the relation between philosophy and politics, he is at the same time implicitly refusing to follow along the path of any of these four figures:

1. Insofar as politics is a condition of philosophy, on a par with art or science, philosophy cannot claim to define the normative ideals to be put into actual practice.

2. Insofar as politics is a truth procedure, or what Badiou always refers to as a *pensée-faire*, or 'thought-practice', it need not wait for the speculative philosopher in order to define the essence of the political or the concept of the impolitical.

3. Insofar as politics here always means active, combative or militant politics, we are outside the realm of contrasting regimes of power, especially state power, with which modern political philosophy preferably entertains itself.

4. Yet politics does not for this reason remain locked within the sphere of an unthinkable or paradoxical practice, as part of an ongoing resistance to theory, which nowadays is becoming openly antiphilosophical. Instead, philosophy does have a role to play according to Badiou. But what role?

In a long – by far the longest – endnote to his last major work, *Logics of Worlds*, which is the follow-up volume to *Being and Event*, Badiou explains that the proper criteria for evaluating the relation between philosophy and politics are those of formal compatibility. 'That which has been thought and invoked as a condition by a philosophy is reconceived in such a way that it becomes another thought, even though it may be the only other (philosophical) thought *compatible* with the initial conditioning thought', Badiou writes.

In short, the relation of philosophy to other kinds of thought [such as politics qua thought-practice] cannot be evaluated in terms of identity or contradiction, neither from its own point of view nor from that of these other kinds of thought. Rather, it is a matter of knowing what it is that – as an effect of conceptual sublimations (or speculative formalisations) – remains essentially compatible with the philosophy in question, and what is instead organically alien to it.[7]

Philosophy for Badiou thus renders the truths of militant politics compatible with those produced in contemporary artistic experiments or scientific innovations. In the words of *Manifesto for Philosophy*, it seeks out a space of compossibility for the truths of its own time. Therein lies the only service – not of goods, but of truths – that philosophy is capable of performing. 'Philosophical concepts weave a general space in which thought accedes to time, to *its* time, so long as the truth procedures of this time find shelter for their compossibility within it', writes Badiou. 'The appropriate metaphor is thus not of the register of addition, not even of systematic reflection. It is rather of the liberty of movement, of a moving-itself of thought within the articulated element of a state of its conditions.'[8] A period or moment of philosophy, therefore, is defined by the relative stability of the operators with which it manages to think together the

-----

7   Alain Badiou, *Logics of Worlds, Being and Event, 2*, trans. Alberto Toscano (London: Continuum, 2009), p. 521.
8   Alain Badiou, *Manifesto for Philosophy*, trans. and introduced by Norman Madarasz (Albany, NY: SUNY Press, 1999), p. 38.

different truth procedures of its time. In particular, Badiou proposes to interrogate the persistence or exhaustion of the modern period of philosophy by focusing on the category of the subject: 'Does the act of proposing, for our time, a space of compossibility within thought of the truths which prolif- erate there, demand the maintenance and usage of the cate- gory of Subject, even profoundly altered and subverted? Or, on the contrary, is our time one in which thought demands the deconstruction of this category?'[9] Badiou's interrogation of the figure of the soldier, in the second talk included here, in large part corresponds to such an investigation into the promises and limits of certain names for the political subject in the modern period, as formalised within the space of philosophy but in constant dialogue with other, nonphilo- sophical domains such as poetry or mathematics.

In fact, the concrete framing of the question of the rela- tionship between philosophy and politics in the following set of talks proceeds by way of a double triangulation. Badiou thus proposes to tackle the obscure knot between politics, democracy and philosophy by creating a certain liberty of movement between politics and two other conditions of philosophy, which are art and science. More specifically, he puts to the test a certain traditional – classical or Marxist – view of militant politics by introducing a playful interaction between politics, poetry and mathematics.

In the case of poetry, this dialogue among the condi- tions of philosophy produces a powerful new reading of the

---

9   Ibid., p. 44.

figure of the soldier emblematised in the romantic and post-romantic poetry of Gerard Manley Hopkins and Wallace Stevens; and in the case of mathematics, we obtain a suggestive transversal dialogue between the notions of the generic respectively invoked by the young Marx in his *Philosophic and Economic Manuscripts of 1844* and in the set-theoretical innovations of Paul Cohen in the 1960s.

3

One final comment might be in order to explain the possible uses of the category of the 'militant' in the title of this collection. While ordinarily this category carries echoes of stomping army boots and the whole arsenal of modern weaponry, such vulgar military connotations need not be the most relevant here. Perhaps equally important is the popular etymology that links the old Latin *miles* to *mill(ia)-ites* or *millia passuum euntes* – that is, 'mile-goers'.[10] We could thus say that a militant, simply put, is somebody who not only talks the talk but also walks the walk, or who goes the full mile.

What is more, perhaps there exists a need here to expand upon Badiou's rather cursory remarks about the ways in which the aristocratic figure of the warrior and the democratic figure of the soldier respectively find expression in epic and lyric poetry. Does this millenarian jump from

---

10   See Roland G. Kent, 'The Etymology of Latin Miles', *Transactions and Proceedings of the American Philological Association* 41 (1910), pp. 5–9.

Homeric epic to post-romantic lyric poetry – all in the name of a quest for a new great fiction – not leapfrog over the quintessential source of early modern fiction in the realm of narrative prose? After all, in late medieval Latin, *miles* even became synonymous with knight-errant. Could we not say then that between the warrior and the soldier, the militant as knight-errant opened up a third figure – with all the charming Quixotry that is perhaps not foreign to Badiou's very own style and wandering spirit in the talks that follow?[11]

---

11   Many key metaphors in *Being and Event* also carry strong echoes from the chivalric and early-modern prose genres that would eventually produce the novel. It is perhaps no coincidence that Badiou constantly speaks of the 'errancy' of being, of the excess of being that 'wanders' like a 'ghost' or 'phantom' in any state of the situation, or of the 'advent' or 'adventure' of the event. For an initial commentary on this aspect of Badiou's work, see Simone Pinet, 'On the Subject of Fiction: Islands and the Emergence of the Novel', *diacritics* 33 (2003), pp. 173–87. Aside from being a novelist himself, Badiou also started his career as a philosopher with an article on the theory of the novel, but subsequently, aside from book reviews about the novels of his friend and fellow-militant Natacha Michel, does not seem to have reflected further upon the importance of the history of prose fiction for his philosophy as a whole. For the early theory of the novelistic element, see Alain Badiou, 'The Autonomy of the Aesthetic Process', in *The Age of the Poets and Other Writings on Twentieth-Century Poetry and Prose*, ed. and trans. Bruno Bosteels (London: Verso, 2014).

Chapter One

The Enigmatic Relationship Between Philosophy and Politics

Before broaching the paradoxical relationship between philosophy and politics, I would like to raise a few simple questions about the future of philosophy itself.

I will begin with a reference to one of my masters, Louis Althusser. For Althusser, the birth of Marxism is not a simple matter. It depends on two revolutions, on two major intellectual events. First, a scientific event, namely, the creation by Marx of a science of history, the name of which is 'historical materialism'. The second event is philosophical in nature and concerns the creation, by Marx and some others, of a new tendency in philosophy, the name of which is 'dialectical materialism'.[1] We can say that a new philosophy is called for to clarify and help with the birth of a new science. Thus, Plato's philosophy was summoned by the beginning of mathematics, or Kant's philosophy by Newtonian physics. There is nothing particularly difficult in all this. But in this context it becomes possible to make a few small remarks about the future of philosophy.

---

1 *Translator's Note*: For Badiou's earliest assessment of the canonical writings of Louis Althusser, see Alain Badiou, 'The (Re) commencement of Dialectical Materialism', in *The Adventure of French Philosophy*, ed. and trans. Bruno Bosteels (London: Verso, 2012), pp. 133–70.

We can begin by considering the fact that this future does not depend principally on philosophy and on its history, but on new facts in certain domains, which are not immediately philosophical in nature. In particular, it depends on facts that belong to the domain of science: for example, mathematics for Plato, Descartes or Leibniz; physics for Kant, Whitehead or Popper; history for Hegel or Marx; biology for Nietzsche, Bergson or Deleuze.

I am perfectly in agreement with the statement that philosophy depends on certain nonphilosophical domains, which I have proposed to call the 'conditions' of philosophy. I merely want to recall that I do not limit the conditions of philosophy to the comings and goings of science. I propose a much vaster ensemble of conditions, pertaining to four different types: science, to be sure, but also politics, art and love. Thus, my work depends, for instance, on a new concept of the infinite, but also on new forms of revolutionary politics, on the great poems by Mallarmé, Rimbaud, Pessoa, Mandelstam or Wallace Stevens, on the prose of Samuel Beckett, and on the new figures of love that have emerged in the context of psychoanalysis, as well as on the complete transformation of all questions concerning sexuation and gender.

We could thus say that the future of philosophy depends on its capacity for progressive adaptation to the changing of its conditions. And, if this is indeed the case, we could say that philosophy always comes in the second place; it always arrives *après-coup*, or in the aftermath, of nonphilosophical innovations.

It is true that this is also Hegel's conclusion. For him philosophy is the bird of wisdom, and the bird of wisdom is the owl. But the owl takes flight only towards the end of the day. Philosophy is the discipline that comes after the day of knowledge, after the day of real-life experiments – when night falls. Apparently, our problem concerning the future of philosophy is thereby solved. We can imagine two cases. First case: a new dawn of creative experiments in matters of science, politics, art or love is on the verge of breaking and we will have the experience of a new evening for philosophy. Second case: our civilisation is exhausted, and the future that we are capable of imagining is a sombre one, a future of perpetual obscurity. The future of philosophy will thus lie in dying its slow death at night. Philosophy will be reduced to what we can read at the beginning of that splendid text by Samuel Beckett, *Company*: 'A voice comes to one in the dark'.[2] A voice with neither meaning nor destination.

And, in fact, from Hegel to Auguste Comte, all the way to Nietzsche, Heidegger or Derrida, without forgetting Wittgenstein and Carnap, we find time and again the philosophical idea of a probable death of philosophy – in any case the death of philosophy in its classical or metaphysical form. Will I, as someone who is well-known for his contempt for the dominant form of our time and his staunch criticism of capitalo-parliamentarianism, preach the necessary end and

---

2   *Translator's Note*: See Samuel Beckett, *Nohow On: Company, Ill Seen Ill Said, Worstward Ho: Three Novels* (New York: Grove Press, 1996), p. 3.

overcoming of philosophy? You know that such is not my position. Quite the contrary, I am attached to the possibility that philosophy, as I already wrote in my first *Manifesto for Philosophy*, must take 'one more step'.[3]

This is because the widespread thesis about the death of metaphysics, the postmodern thesis of an overcoming of the philosophical element as such by way of novel, more hybridised, and more mixed, less dogmatic intellectualities – this thesis runs into a whole series of difficulties.

The first difficulty, which is perhaps overly formal, is the following: for a long time now the idea of the end of philosophy has been a typically philosophical idea. Moreover, it is often a positive idea. For Hegel, philosophy has reached its end because it is capable of grasping what is absolute knowledge. For Marx, philosophy, as interpretation of the world, may be replaced by a concrete transformation of this same world. For Nietzsche, negative abstraction represented by the old philosophy must be destroyed to liberate the genuine vital affirmation, the great 'Yes!' to all that exists. And the analytical tendency, the metaphysical phrases, which are pure nonsense, must be deconstructed in favour of clear propositions and statements, under the paradigm of modern logic.

In all these cases we see how the great declarations about the death of philosophy in general, or of metaphysics in

---

3 *Translator's Note*: See Alain Badiou, *Manifesto for Philosophy*, trans. and introduced by Norman Madarasz (Albany, NY: SUNY Press, 1999), p. 32.

particular, are most likely the rhetorical means to introduce a new path, a new aim, within philosophy itself. The best way to say 'I am a new philosopher' is probably to say with great emphasis: 'Philosophy is over, philosophy is dead! Therefore, I propose that with me there begins something entirely new. Not philosophy, but thinking! Not philosophy, but the force of life! Not philosophy, but a new rational language! In fact, not the old philosophy, but the new philosophy, which by some amazing chance happens to be mine.'

It is not impossible that the future of philosophy always takes the form of a resurrection. The old philosophy, like the old man, is dead; but this death is in fact the birth of the new man, of the new philosopher.

However, there exists a close relationship between resurrection and immortality, between the greatest imaginable change, the passage from death to life, and the most complete absence of change imaginable, when we place ourselves in the joy of salvation.

Perhaps the repetition of the motif of the end of philosophy joined with the repeated motif of a new beginning of thought is the sign of a fundamental immobility of philosophy as such. It is possible that philosophy must always place its continuity, its repetitive nature, under the rubric of the dramatic pair of birth and death.

At this point, we can come back to the work of Althusser. It is Althusser who argues that philosophy depends on science, all the while making an extremely strange argument, namely, that philosophy has no history at all, that philosophy is always the same thing. In this case, the problem of the future of philosophy in fact becomes a simple one: the future of philosophy is its past.

It boggles the mind to see Althusser, the great Marxist, become the last defender of the old scholastic notion of a *philosophia perennis*, of a philosophy as the pure repetition of the same, a philosophy in the Nietzschean style as eternal return of the same.

But what does this 'same' really mean? What is this sameness of the same that is equivalent to the ahistorical destiny of philosophy? This question obviously brings us back to the old discussion on the true nature of philosophy. Roughly, we can distinguish two tendencies in this debate. For the first tendency, philosophy is essentially a reflexive mode of knowledge: the knowledge of truth in the theoretical domain, the knowledge of values in the practical domain. And we must organise the process whereby these two fundamental forms of knowledge are acquired and transmitted. Thus, the form that is appropriate for philosophy is that of the school. The philosopher then is a professor, like Kant, Hegel, Husserl, Heidegger and so many others, myself included. The philosopher organises the reasoned transmission and discussion of questions concerning truth and values. Indeed, it belongs to philosophy to have invented the form of the school, since at least the Greeks.

The second possibility holds that philosophy is not really a form of knowledge, whether theoretical or practical. Rather, it consists in the direct transformation of a subject, being a radical conversion of sorts – a complete upheaval of existence. Consequently, philosophy comes very close to religion, even though its means are exclusively rational; it comes very close to love, but without the violent support of desire; very close to political commitment, but without the constraint of a centralised organisation; very close to artistic creation, but without the sensible means of art; very close to scientific knowledge, but without the formalism of mathematics or the empirical and technical means of physics. For this second tendency, philosophy is not necessarily a subject-matter belonging to the school, to pedagogy, to professors and the problem of transmission. It is a free address of someone to someone else. Like Socrates addressing the youth in the streets of Athens, like Descartes writing letters to Princess Elisabeth of Bohemia, like Jean-Jacques Rousseau writing his *Confessions*; or like the poems of Nietzsche, the novels and plays of Jean-Paul Sartre; or, if you allow me this touch of narcissism, like my own theatrical or novelistic works, as well as the affirmative and combative style that infuses, I believe, even the most complex of my philosophical writings.

In other words, we can conceive of philosophy, to speak like Lacan, as a form of the discourse of the University, an affair for philosophers and students in reasonable institutions. This is the perennially scholastic vision of Aristotle. Or else we can conceive of philosophy as the most radical form of the discourse of the Master, an affair of personal commitment in which the combative affirmation comes first (above all against the sophists and against the doubts of the sages who honour the University).

In this second view of things, philosophy is no more knowledge than it is knowledge of knowledge. It is an action.

We could say that what identifies philosophy are not the rules of a discourse but the singularity of an act. It is this act that the enemies of Socrates designated as 'corrupting the youth'. And, as you know, this is the reason why Socrates was condemned to death. 'To corrupt the youth' is, after all, a very apt name to designate the philosophical act, provided that we understand the meaning of 'corruption'. To corrupt here means to teach the possibility of refusing all blind submission to established opinions. To corrupt means to give the youth certain means to change their opinion with regard to social norms, to substitute debate and rational critique for imitation and approval, and even, if the question is a matter of principle, to substitute revolt for obedience. But this revolt is neither spontaneous nor aggressive, to the extent that it is the consequence of principles and of a critique offered for the discussion of all.

In Rimbaud's poetry we find the strange expression: 'logical revolts'.[4] This is probably a good definition of the philosophical act. It is not by chance that my old friend–enemy, the remarkable antiphilosopher Jacques Rancière, created in the 1970s a very important journal, which carried precisely the title *Les Révoltes logiques*.[5]

---

4   *Translator's Note*: See Arthur Rimbaud, 'Democracy', *Complete Works, Selected Letters*, trans. and introduced by Wallace Fowlie, rev. edn by Seth Whidden (Chicago: University of Chicago Press, 2005), p. 351.

5   *Translator's Note*: Selections of Jacques Rancière's writings for the journal *Les Révoltes logiques* have been collected and translated as *Staging the People: The Proletarian and His Double*, trans.

But if the true essence of philosophy consists in being an act, we understand better why, in the eyes of Louis Althusser, there exists no real history of philosophy. In his own work, Althusser proposes that the active function of philosophy consists in introducing a division among opinions. To be more precise, a division among the opinions about scientific knowledge – or, more generally, among theoretical activities. What kind of division? It is ultimately the division between materialism and idealism. As a Marxist, Althusser thought that materialism was the revolutionary framework for theoretical activities and that idealism was the conservative framework. Thus, his final definition was the following: philosophy is like a political struggle in the theoretical field.[6]

But, independently of this Marxist conclusion, we can make two remarks:

1. The philosophical act always takes the form of a decision, a separation, a clear distinction. Between knowledge and opinion, between correct and false opinions, between truth and falsity, between Good and Evil, between wisdom and madness, between the affirmative position and the purely critical position, and so on.

David Fernbach (London: Verso, 2011); and *The Intellectual and His People: Staging the People, Volume 2*, trans. David Fernbach (London: Verso, 2012).

6   *Translator's Note*: See, in particular, Louis Althusser, *Lenin and Philosophy and Other Essays* (London: Monthly Review Press, 2001).

2. The philosophical act always has a normative dimension. The division is also a hierarchy. In the case of Marxism, the good term is materialism and the bad one, idealism. But, more generally, we see that the division introduced among the concepts or experiences is in fact always a way of imposing a new hierarchy, especially for the youth. And, from a negative standpoint, the result is the intellectual overturning of an established order and an old hierarchy.

So, in philosophy, we have something invariant, something of the order of a compulsion to repeat, or like the eternal return of the same. But this invariance is of the order of the act, and not of knowledge. It is a subjectivity, for which knowing in all its forms is only one means among others.

Philosophy is the act of reorganising all theoretical and practical experiments by proposing a great new normative division, which inverts an established intellectual order and promotes new values beyond the commonly accepted ones. The form all this takes is of a more or less free address to each and everyone, but first and foremost to the youth, because a philosopher knows perfectly well that young people are the ones who must make decisions about their lives and who are most often ready to accept the risks of a logical revolt.

All this explains why philosophy is to some extent always the same thing. Of course, all philosophers think that their work is absolutely new. This is only human. A number of historians of philosophy have introduced absolute breaks. For example, after Descartes, it is evident that metaphysics must take modern science as the paradigm of its rational construction. After Kant, classical metaphysics is declared impossible. Or, after Wittgenstein, it is forbidden to forget that the study of language constitutes the very core of philosophy. We thus have a rationalist turn, a critical turn, a linguistic turn. But, in fact, nothing in philosophy is irreversible. There is no absolute turn. Numerous philosophers today are capable of finding in Plato or Leibniz far more interesting and stimulating points than the points of seemingly comparable intensity found in Heidegger or in Wittgenstein. This is because their matrix is by and large identical to that of Plato or Leibniz. The immanent affinities that exist among philosophers can be explained only by the fact that philosophy is a repetition of its act. Deleuze with Leibniz and Spinoza; Sartre with Descartes and Hegel; Merleau-Ponty with Bergson and Aristotle; myself with Plato and Hegel; Slavoj Žižek with Kant and Schelling. And, possibly, for almost 3,000 years, everyone with everyone else.

But if the philosophical act is formally the same, and the return of the same, we will have to account for the change in historical context. For the act takes place under certain conditions. When a philosopher proposes a new division and a new hierarchy for the experiments of his or her time, it is because a new intellectual creation, a new truth, has just made its appearance. It is in fact because, in his or her eyes, we have to assume the consequences of a new event within the actual conditions of philosophy.

Some examples. Plato proposed a division between the sensible and the intelligible under the conditions of the geometry of Eudoxus and of a post-Pythagorean concept of number and measure. Hegel introduced history and becoming into the absolute Idea, on the account of the striking novelty of the French Revolution. Nietzsche developed a dialectical relation between Greek tragedy and the birth of philosophy in the context of the tumultuous feelings that the discovery of Wagner's musical drama awoke in him. And Derrida transformed the classical approach of rigid metaphysical oppositions, largely on account of the growing and unavoidable importance, for our experiences, of the feminine dimension.

This is why we can finally speak of a creative repetition. There is something invariant, which takes the form of a gesture, a gesture of division. And there is, under the pressure of certain events and their consequences, the need to transform certain aspects of the philosophical gesture. We thus have a form, and we have the variable form of the unique form. This explains why we can clearly recognise philosophy and the philosophers, in spite of their enormous differences and their violent conflicts. Kant said that the history of philosophy was a battlefield. He was absolutely right. But it is also the repetition of the same battle, in the same field. A musical image may be helpful here. The becoming of philosophy has the classical form of the theme and its variations. The repetition provides the theme, and the constant novelty, the variations.

And all this takes place after certain events in politics, in art, in science, in love: events that have given rise to the need for a new variation on the same theme. Thus, there is some truth to Hegel's statement. It is indeed the case that we philosophers work at night, after the day of the true becoming of a new truth. I am reminded of a splendid poem by Wallace Stevens – whose title, 'Man Carrying Thing', resembles that of a painting – in which Stevens writes: 'We must endure our thoughts all night'. Alas, such is the fate of philosophers and of philosophy. And Stevens continues: 'until the bright obvious stands motionless in cold.'[7] Yes, we hope, we believe that one day the 'bright obvious' will rise up motionless, in the stellar coldness of its ultimate form. It will be the last stage of philosophy, the absolute Idea, the complete revelation. But this does not come to pass. To the contrary, when something happens during the day of living truths, we have to repeat the philosophical act and create a new variation.

In this way, the future of philosophy, like its past, is a creative repetition. It will forever be the case that we must endure our thoughts for as long as the night lasts.

Among such nocturnal thoughts, none is probably more worrying for us today than those that are tied to the political condition. And the reason for this is simple: politics itself stands by and large in a kind of night of thought. But the philosopher cannot resign himself so as to let this nocturnal position be the result of a night of concrete truths. The philosopher must try to discern far into the distance,

---

7   *Translator's Note*: See Wallace Stevens, 'Man Carrying Thing', in *The Collected Poems of Wallace Stevens* (New York: Vintage, 1990), p. 351.

towards the horizon, whatever the glowing lights announce.
This time the philosopher is rather like the watchman from
the beginning of Aeschylus's *Agamemnon*. You know this
unsurpassed passage:

> Now as this bed stricken with night and drenched with
> dew I keep, I lie awake, without respite, like a watchdog
> to mark the grand processionals of all the stars of night
> burdened with winter and again with heat for men. Of
> these dynasties in their shining blazoned on the air,
> I have come to know the science of these stars upon
> their wane and when the rest arise.

The philosopher is the subject of this kind of science; when
night falls he is the loyal watchdog of the Outside. But his
joy is made of the announcement of dawn. Still Aeschylus:
'Now let there be again redemption from distress, the flare
burning from the blackness in good augury.'[8]

These last weeks, precisely, our country once more has
seen proof that there exists a popular disposition to invent
at night a few new forms of dawn.[9] Perhaps we possess at

---

8 *Translator's Note*: See Aeschylus, *Agamemnon*, in *Oresteia*,
trans. Richmond Lattimore (Chicago: University of Chicago Press,
1953), p. 35. Since Badiou's prose version combines several of the
opening lines from the watchman in *Agamemnon*, I have somewhat
freely adapted the English translation to reflect Badiou's usage.

9 *Translator's Note:* Speaking in October 2010, Badiou is
making reference to the widespread and militant opposition, albeit
unsuccessful, to the Sarkozy government's pension reforms.

least the flames of the possible fire of joy. The philosopher, naturally, lying down on his bed drenched in dew, opens one eye. And he enumerates the lights.

You know that there exist four great ensembles in our population from which, if we limit ourselves to the last two decades, we can expect that they may escape the gloomy discipline of the current state of affairs. We know this, since each of these collectives, in the politically limited but historically assured form of the mass movement, has given proof of a form of existence that is irreducible to the games of the economy and the State.

Let us name the schooled youth who, worried about their future, not so long ago were victorious on the question of the CPE.[10] This is a lively and self-assured movement – a victory that is no doubt equivocal, but a promising subjectivity nonetheless.

Let us name the popular youth, harassed by the police and stigmatised by society, whose riots periodically fire up the masses in the impoverished neighbourhoods or *cités*, and whose obscure rebellious obstinacy, rising up from times immemorial and governed only by the imperative 'it is

---

10   *Translator's Note*: Badiou is referring to the massive protests of February–April 2006 in France against the 'first employment contract', or *contrat de première embauche* (CPE), approved as part of then–Prime Minister Dominique de Villepin's labour deregulation policies. Eventually, after more than a million people took to the streets throughout the country, many of them young people and students, the law was scrapped by President Jacques Chirac.

just to revolt', has at least the merit of making the well-to-do people tremble with fear.[11]

Let us name the mass of ordinary wage labourers, capable of holding steady for days in the midst of winter, under the sole watchword of 'together, all together', gathering in immense assemblies and mobilising up to one-third of the total population all the way into certain small towns in the provinces.[12]

Let us finally name the newly arrived proletarians from Africa, Asia, Eastern Europe, situated as always since the nineteenth century at the strategic centre of genuine politics, with or without legal papers, knowing how to organise, protest, occupy, in the long war of resistance for their rights.

---

11   *Translator's Note*: On the Maoist slogan 'it is just to revolt' or 'it is right to rebel', see also Alain Badiou, 'An Essential Philosophical Thesis: "It Is Right To Rebel against the Reactionaries"', trans. Alberto Toscano, *positions: east asia cultures critique* 13 (2005), pp. 669–77.

12   *Translator's Note*: *Tous ensemble* ('all together', but for Badiou *ensemble* also always carries a ring of set theory, or *théorie des ensembles*) was the slogan (chanted as *Tous ensemble! Tous ensemble! Ouais! Ouais!*) of, among others, the December 1995 strikes in France against the plan of then–Prime Minister Alain Juppé for the reform of pensions and social security. Widely considered the most significant strikes in France since May 1968, their watchword would eventually be co-opted, first into a hit single by the French singer Johnny Hallyday and then, even more perversely, in the electoral campaign for soon-to-be President Nicolas Sarkozy, as the anti-1968 slogan *Ensemble, tout est possible* ('Together, everything is possible').

We know that the smallest linkage among these ensembles, anything that may produce their inseparation, will open a new sequence of political invention. The State has no other major task except to prohibit, by all possible means, including violent ones, any connection, even limited, between the popular youth of the 'cities' and the students, between the students and the mass of ordinary salaried workers, among the latter and the newly arrived proletarians, and even, despite its apparent naturalness, any connection between the popular youth and the proletarian newcomers, between sons and fathers. Besides, this was the point of the ideology of 'Touche pas à mon pote',[13] made up of 'youth-ism' and contempt for the working condition to which the fathers had been assigned and in which they had been able to show their strength, during a few major strikes in the 1970s and the early 1980s.

The only connection that has been able to last is the one that gathers militant intellectuals and proletarian newcomers. Here there are experiments going on that take the form of a restricted action, offering the resources for a political long march that would owe nothing to the parliamentary and syndicalist sham.

The most recent shimmer of light that the philosopher's eye can perceive is that attempts are being made to experiment

---

13   *Translator's Note*: *Touche pas à mon pote* ('Hands off my mate'), the slogan printed on thousands of yellow hand logos, was the watchword of the French anti-racist NGO, SOS Racisme, founded in 1984 and closely tied to the French Socialist Party, and often criticised by the radical left as a weak-kneed and depoliticised recuperation of anti-racism.

precisely with connections of this kind – connections that the united front of State, unions and party leadership, with the 'Left' ahead of the pack, are trying hard to proscribe. Certain composite groups are forming and assigning themselves a set of precise tasks: occupy this or that, create a vengeful banner, breathe life into the trail of syndicalist inertia . . . So, then, perhaps today, or tomorrow . . .

Let us in any case greet what is happening, this determination of sorts in doing away with the emblem of state corruption, about which I may at least be credited for having said very early on to what extent it is harmful and of what, in this sense, it is the name.

In light of all this, I come back to reflect anew on the strange connection, which I have experienced at a deeply personal level, between politics and philosophy.

I will begin by noting a striking contradiction. On the one hand, philosophy is clearly and necessarily a democratic activity. I will explain why. On the other hand, the political conceptions of the majority of philosophers, from Plato to myself, including Hegel, Nietzsche, Wittgenstein, Heidegger and Deleuze, have nothing democratic about them in the usual sense of the word. In other words: philosophers in general do not recognise the unanimously celebrated virtues of the parliamentary State and freedom of opinion.

We thus have a contradiction between the true nature of philosophy, which is certainly a democratic conception of intellectual argument and free thinking, and the explicit conceptions of philosophy in the field of politics, which accept very often the existence of an authoritarian framing for the collective destiny of humanity, and in any case feel no kind of fascination for the type of political regime that today dominates the West.

There is something like a paradoxical relationship between three terms: democracy, politics and philosophy. We must pass from democracy to philosophy. In fact, such is the road followed in the creation of philosophy among the ancient Greeks. The birth of philosophy is evidently dependent on the invention by the Greeks of the first form of democratic power. But we must also pass from philosophy to politics. In fact, politics most certainly has always been one of the principal preoccupations of philosophers throughout the entire history of the becoming of philosophy. But, even as politics constitutes an object of reflection for philosophy, it is in general very difficult to pass from this kind of politics to democracy.

Democracy, one might say, is a necessity at the source of philosophy and a difficulty at its far end.

Our question thus becomes: What is it in politics that is modified by the philosophical act in such a way that democracy begins by being a necessity, only to become something impossible or obscure in the end?

Our answer will be that the difficulty is situated in the relation between the democratic notion of freedom or liberty and the philosophical concept of truth. In short, if there exists something like a political truth, this truth is an obligation for any rational spirit. As a result, freedom is absolutely limited. Conversely, if there exists no limitation of this order, there exists no political truth. But in that case there is no positive relationship between philosophy and politics.

The three terms – politics, democracy and philosophy – are, finally, linked by the question of truth. The obscure knot is in fact determined by the obscurity that is proper to the category of truth. The problem then becomes: What is a democratic conception of truth? What is, in opposition to relativism and scepticism, the democratic universality? What is a political rule that applies to all, but without the constraint of transcendence?

But let us begin at the beginning, with the following two points:

1. Why is democracy a condition for the existence of philosophy?
2. Why is philosophy so often ill-suited for a democratic vision of politics?

Philosophy has two fundamental characteristics. On the one hand, it is a discourse independent of the place occupied by the one who speaks. If you prefer: philosophy is the discourse of neither king nor priest, of neither prophet nor god. There is no guarantee for the philosophical discourse on the side of transcendence, power or sacred function. Philosophy assumes that the search for truth is open to all. The philosopher can be anyone. What the philosopher says is validated (or not) not by the speaker's position, but solely by the spoken content. Or, more technically, the philosophical evaluation is not concerned with the subjective enunciation, but solely with the objectively enunciated. Philosophy is a discourse whose legitimacy stems only from itself.

Therein lies a clearly democratic feature. Philosophy is completely indifferent to the social, cultural or religious position of the one who speaks or thinks. It accepts that it can come from anyone. And philosophy is exposed to approval or critique, without any prior selection of those who approve or object. It consents to be for anyone whatsoever.

We can thus conclude that it belongs to the essence of philosophy to be democratic. But we ought not to forget that philosophy, which consents to be totally universal in its origin as well as in its address, could not consent to be democratic in the same sense as far as its objectives, or its destination, are concerned. Anyone can be a philosopher, or the interlocutor of a philosopher. But it is not true that any opinion is worth as much as any other opinion. The axiom of the equality of intelligences is far from constituting an axiom of the equality of opinions. Since the beginning of philosophy, we must follow Plato in distinguishing, first, between correct and mistaken opinions, and, secondly, between opinion and truth. To the extent that the ultimate aim of philosophy is thoroughly to clarify the distinction between truth and opinion, evidently there can be no genuine philosophical interpretation of the great democratic principle of the freedom of opinion. Philosophy opposes the unity and universality of truth to the plurality and relativity of opinions.

There is another factor that limits the democratic tendency of philosophy. Philosophy is certainly exposed to critical

judgment. But this exposure implies the acceptance of a
common rule for discussion. We must recognise the validity
of the arguments. And finally we must accept the existence
of a universal logic as the formal condition of the axiom of
the equality of intelligences. Metaphorically speaking, this is
the 'mathematical' dimension of philosophy: there exists a
freedom of address, but there is also the need for a strict rule
for discussion.

Exactly like mathematics, philosophy is valid from all and
for all, and knows no specific language. But there is a strict
rule that applies to the consequences.

Thus, when philosophy examines politics it cannot do
so according to a line of pure liberty or freedom, much less
according to the principle of the freedom of opinion; it treats
of the question of what a political truth can be. Or again: it
treats of the question of what politics is when it obeys the
following two principles:

1. Compatibility with the philosophical principle of
the equality of intelligences.
2. Compatibility with the philosophical principle of
the subordination of the variety of opinions to the
universality of truth.

We can say simply that equality and universality are the
characteristics of a valid politics in the field of philosophy.
The classical name for this is justice. Justice means exam-
ining any situation from the point of view of an egalitarian
norm vindicated as universal.

One will note that, in the idea of justice, equality is far more important than liberty, and universality far more important than particularity, identity or individuality. This is because there is a problem with the current definition of democracy as representative of individual liberties.

Richard Rorty has declared: 'Democracy is more important than philosophy.'[14] With this political principle, Rorty in fact prepares the dissolution of philosophy into cultural relativism. But Plato, at the start of philosophy, says the exact opposite: philosophy is far more important than democracy. And if justice is the philosophical name of politics as truth of the collective, then justice is more important than freedom.

The great critique of democratic politics that we find in Plato is slightly ambiguous. On the one hand, it is certainly an aristocratic personal opinion. But, on the other hand, it presents a genuine problem – that of a kind of contradiction, which can become antagonistic, between justice and liberty.

To acquire some insight into this, we can read the deliberations among the French revolutionaries between 1792 and 1794. The daunting notion of 'terror' intervenes exactly at the point where the universality that is supposed to be at work behind the political truth enters into a violent conflict with

---

14   *Translator's Note*: See for example Richard Rorty, 'The Priority of Democracy to Philosophy', in *Objectivity, Relativism, and Truth: Philosophical Papers, Volume 1* (Cambridge: CUP, 1991), pp. 175–96.

the particularity of interests. Subjectively, the great revolutionaries of the period translate this conflict by saying that where virtue fails, terror is inevitable. But what is virtue? It is the political will, or what Saint-Just calls 'public consciousness', which unflinchingly puts equality above purely individual liberty, and the universality of principles above the interests of particulars.

This debate is by no means outdated. What, indeed, is our situation today – I mean, the situation of the people who are comfortable enough to call themselves 'Westerners'? The price to be paid for our cherished liberty, here in the Western world, is that of a monstrous inequality, first within our own countries but then, above all, abroad. From a philosophical point of view, there exists no justice whatsoever in the contemporary world. From this point of view, we are entirely without virtue in the sense given to this word by our great ancestors the Jacobins. But we also flatter ourselves for not being terrorists either. Now, again, Saint-Just also asked: 'What do the people want who want neither virtue nor terror?' And his answer to this question was: they want corruption. There is indeed a desire for us to wallow in corruption without looking any further. Here, what I call 'corruption' refers not so much to the shameful trafficking, the exchanges between banditry and 'decent society', the embezzlements of all kinds, for which we know that the capitalist economy serves as the support. By 'corruption' I mean, above all, the mental corruption which leads to a world that, while being so evidently devoid of any principle, presents itself as, and is assumed by the majority of those who benefit from it to be, the best of all possible worlds. This reaches the point where, in the name of this corrupt world, people tolerate the waging of wars against those who would revolt against such disgusting self-satisfaction – and, within our borders, our persecution of those who are badly 'inte-grated', all those who, having arrived from elsewhere, do not unconditionally profess the self-proclaimed superiority of capitalo-parliamentarianism.

Brought up in a world whose thinking is corrupt, and in which injustice is a principle both secret and supremely sacred, rising up against this corruption with all the means available, philosophers should not be surprised to see that they have to live in a paradoxical situation. Democracy is a condition for philosophy, but philosophy has no direct relation to justice. Justice rather presents itself, at the farthest remove from the democratic and corrupt delights of individual liberty, as the contingent alliance between virtue and terror. Now, justice is the philosophical name of truth in the domain of politics. Thus, the knot of the three terms – philosophy, democracy and politics – remains an obscure one.

I will now make a classical detour through mathematics. Mathematics is probably the best paradigm of justice that one can find, as Plato was able to show very early on. In mathematics we have first of all a kind of primitive liberty, which is the liberty of the choice of axioms. But after that, we have a total determination, based on the rules of logic. We must therefore accept all the consequences of our first choice. And this acceptance does not amount to a form of liberty; it is a constraint, a necessity: finding the correct proof is a very hard intellectual labour. In the end, all this strictly forms a universal equality in a precise sense: a proof is a proof for anyone whatsoever, without exception, who accepts the primitive choice and the logical rules. Thus, we obtain the notions of choice, consequences, equality and universality.

What we have here is in fact the paradigm of classical revolutionary politics, whose goal is justice. One must begin by accepting a fundamental choice. In the historical sequence which goes from the great Jacobins of 1792, executed in throngs in 1794 after the 9th Thermidor, to the last storms of the Cultural Revolution in China and the 'leftism' everywhere else in the world – that is, the end of the 1970s – the choice is between what the Chinese revolutionaries call the two 'roads' or the two 'classes': the revolutionary road or the conservative road; the working class or the bourgeoisie; private life or collective action. Then, one must accept the consequences of one's choice – namely, the organisation, the harsh struggles, the sacrifices: this is no freedom of opinion and lifestyles, but discipline and prolonged work to find the strategic means for victory. And the result is not a democratic State in the usual sense of the term, but the dictatorship of the proletariat, aiming to annihilate the resistance of the enemy. At the same time, all this is presented as being entirely universal, because the objective is not the power of a particular class or group, but the end of all classes and all inequalities, and, in the final instance, the end of the State as such.

In this conception, democracy is in fact the name of two completely different things. It is first of all, as Lenin said, the name of a form of the State – the democratic State with its elections, its representatives, its constitutional government and so on. And secondly it is a form of mass action: a popular or active democracy, with large meetings, marches, riots, insurrections and so on. In the first sense, democracy bears no direct relation whatsoever to revolutionary politics or to justice. In the second sense, democracy is neither a norm nor an objective; it is simply a means of promoting an active popular presence in the political field. Democracy is not the political truth itself, but one of the means for finding the political truth.

And yet, philosophy is also democratic, as we saw; it is the condition for a new apprenticeship, a new status of discourse – a status which has no sacred place, no sacred book, which has neither king nor priest, neither prophet nor god as the guarantee of its legitimacy.

We can thus propose a new hypothesis in order for us to grasp this obscure knot in its entirety. From the point of view of philosophy, democracy is neither a norm nor a law nor an objective. Democracy is only one of the possible means of popular emancipation, exactly in the way the mathematical constraints are also a condition of philosophy.

This is why we cannot pass in any self-evident way from philosophy to democracy, and yet democracy is a condition of philosophy. This surely means that the word 'democracy' can take on two different meanings, both at the source and at the endpoint of philosophy. At the source, as formal condition, it designates in fact the submission of all validations of statements to a free proto-col of argumentation, independent of the position of the person who speaks and open to be discussed by anyone whatsoever. At the endpoint, as real democratic move-ment, it designates one of the means of popular emanci-patory politics.

I propose to call 'communism', philosophically speaking, the subjective existence of the unity of these two meanings, the formal and the real. That is to say, it is the hypothesis of a place of thought where the formal condition of philosophy would itself be sustained by the real condition of the exist-ence of a democratic politics wholly different from the actual democratic State. That is, again, the hypothesis of a place where the rule of submission to a free protocol of argumenta-tion, open to be debated by anyone, would have as its source the real existence of emancipatory politics. 'Communism' would be the subjective state in which the liberatory projec-tion of collective action would be somehow indiscernible from the protocols of thinking that philosophy requires in order to exist.

Of course, you will recognise in this a Platonic desire, though expanded from the aristocracy of the guardians to the popular collective in its entirety. This wish could be expressed as follows: wherever a human collective is work-ing in the direction of equality, the conditions are met for everyone to be a philosopher. This is clearly why, in the nine-teenth century, there were so many worker–philosophers, whose existence and will have been so eloquently described by Rancière.[15] It is also why, during the Cultural Revolution in China, one saw the appearance in the factories of workers' circles of dialectical philosophy. We may also quote Bertolt Brecht, for whom the theatre was a possible place, though also an ephemeral one, for emancipation, and who thought of creating a Society of Friends of the Dialectic.[16]

The key to understanding the obscure knot between politics, democracy and philosophy thus lies in the fact that the independence of politics creates the place in which the democratic condition of philosophy undergoes a metamorphosis. In this sense, all emancipatory politics contains for philosophy, whether visible or invisible, the watchword that brings about the actuality of universality – namely: if all are together, then all are communists! And if all are communists, then all are philosophers!

As you know, Plato's fundamental intuition on this point went no farther than to confide the leadership of things to an aristocracy of philosophers who would live an egalitarian, sober, virtuous, communist life. Borrowing a metaphor

---

15   *Translator's Note*: See, among others, Jacques Rancière, *Proletarian Nights: The Workers' Dream in Nineteenth-Century France*, introduced by Donald Reid (London: Verso, 2012).

16   *Translator's Note*: The proposal that Bertolt Brecht discussed with Walter Benjamin, among others, was for the foundation of a Society of Materialist Friends of the Hegelian Dialectic, following the example of Lenin, who had used this expression in a letter published in German in 1922 in the periodical *Die Kommunistische Internationale*. See Erdmut Wizisla, *Walter Benjamin and Bertolt Brecht: The Story of a Friendship*, trans. Christine Shuttleworth (New Haven: Yale University Press, 2009), p. 41.

from Einstein, this is what we could call a restricted communism. The point is to pass in philosophy to a generalised communism. Our city-polis, if this name is still appropriate for the political place constituted by the thought-practice of contemporary politics, will ignore the social differentiation which to Plato seemed inevitable – just as our democratic contemporaries, in the name of 'realism' and terrorised by the idea of Terror, consider it inevitable for there to be property, inheritance, extreme concentration of wealth, division of labour, financial banditry, neocolonial wars, persecution of the poor, and corruption. And, as a result, this city-polis will also ignore the distinction, as far as the universality of philosophy is concerned, between the source and the address. Coming from all as well as the destiny of all: that will define the existence of philosophy insofar as, under the condition of politics, it will be democratic, in the communist sense of the term, both at the source and at the endpoint of its actual existence.

Chapter Two

The Figure of the Soldier

In any period of time, in any sequence of history, it is important that we maintain a relationship with what exceeds our possibilities – with what, as an idea, exists beyond the natural needs of the human animal. In crucial experiences, such as the construction of love, artistic creations, scientific discoveries or political sequences, we are offered the chance of exceeding the limits of our vital and social determinations. Within our own humanity, we must come to terms with the obscure, violent, and – at the same time – luminous and peaceful element of inhumanity within the human element itself. That is why my friend Jean-François Lyotard was able to write that the famous 'human rights' are in fact 'the rights of the infinite'.[1] For humanity, to the extent that the inhuman is a creative part of it, is not reducible to animality. It is in the element of inhumanity that human creation makes appear that part of human 'nature' which does not yet exist but must become. Humanity as a natural totality does not exist, since humanity is identical to the local victories that it obtains over its immanent element of inhumanity.

---

1   *Translator's Note*: See Jean-François Lyotard, *The Differend: Phrases in Dispute*, trans. Georges Van Den Abbeele (Minneapolis: University of Minnesota Press, 1988), p. 31.

To accept and support this experience of the inhuman element within ourselves, we must, all of us, human animals that we are, make use of certain immaterial means. We must create a symbolic representation of this humanity that exists beyond itself, in the fearsome and fertile element of the inhuman. I call that sort of representation a heroic figure. 'Figure', because the type of action that is at stake here is essentially a recognisable form. 'Heroic', because heroism is properly the act of the infinite at work in human actions. 'Heroism' is the luminous appearance, in a concrete situation, of something that assumes its humanity beyond the natural limits of the human animal.

I firmly believe that our current historical moment is disoriented. The previous century was essentially the century of negative heroic orientations. It was defined by a terrible will to support, in the name of a humanity to come, all the forms of its immanent inhumanity. The idea was to create at any cost a new world and a new man. Everywhere there was a call for heroic figures, sometimes frightening and sombre. The word 'revolution' was the synthesis of this destructive experiment: communist revolution, the artistic destruction of all arts, the scientific and technological revolution, the sexual revolution . . . The figure of the end of the old traditions was the heroism of destruction and the creation ex nihilo of a new real. Humanity itself was the new God.

Today, this configuration is in a state of total crisis. One of the symptoms of this crisis is the return of the old traditions and the seeming resurrection of old dead gods. All the heroic figures are old ones too – such as, for example, religious sacrifice and bloody fanaticism. In the guise of these figures, nothing new can occur. They bespeak a disjunction between the human and the inhuman, and not an integration of the inhuman into a new sequence of the historical existence of humanity. But the absence of any sort of heroic figure is certainly of no more value than the old sacrifice. Instead, we have the strict inhumanity of technological murder and the bureaucratic surveillance of all aspects of life. We have bloody wars, or at least police-type wars, including of States against their own people, without the least bit of conviction or faith. In fact, without an active figure involving an element of symbolic creative value, we have only a formless conflict between the old religious sacrifice and the blind will of capitalist control. And everywhere this war has a disorienting effect, which turns important fractions of the popular youth, in particular, into the site of a despair that is devoid of all ideas and a form of nihilism delivered over to the worst.

The fact of disorientation makes it incumbent upon us to think about the fate of heroic figures. Our problem can be formalised in new terms, which as always are those of a seeming dilemma. In disoriented times, we cannot accept the return of the old, deadly figure of religious sacrifice; but neither can we accept the complete lack of any figure, and the complete disappearance of any idea of heroism. The consequence of both hypotheses, indeed, is the end of any dialectical relationship between humanity and its element of inhumanity, and thus the dissolution of any creative dimension in the atonal and violent universe of the management of everything that exists. In both cases, in other words, the result can only be the sad success of what Nietzsche named 'the last man'.[2] 'The last man' is the exhausted figure of a man devoid of any figure. It is the nihilistic image of the fixed nature of the human animal, devoid of all creative possibility of overcoming.

Our task is to find a new heroic figure, which is neither the return of the old figure of religious or national sacrifice nor the nihilistic figure of the last man. Is there a place, in a disoriented world, for a new style of heroism?

But let us begin from the beginning. We must analyse the most important features of the figures during the last historical sequence. I propose to enumerate them as follows:

1. The paradigm of the site of heroism has been war.

2. The paradigm of all heroic figures during the revolutionary sequence, from 1789 (beginning of the French Revolution) until 1976 (end of the Cultural Revolution in China) has been the soldier.

3. This figure of the soldier was a creation of the past two centuries because, in the wars before that, the heroic figure was not the soldier but the warrior.

4. The creative value of the figure of the warrior is illustrated in epic; that of the figure of the soldier in romantic and post-romantic lyric poetry.

5. In contemporary images (movies, television and so on), we can notice nostalgia for the warrior, which is a

---

2   *Translator's Note*: See for instance 'Zarathustra's Prologue', in Friedrich Nietzsche, *Thus Spoke Zarathustra*, eds Adrian Del Caro and Robert Pippin (Cambridge: CUP, 2006), pp. 9–10.

sign of the decomposition of the figure of the soldier, under the pressure of nihilistic individualism.

6. The great problem is to create a paradigm of heroism beyond war, a figure that would be neither that of the warrior nor that of the soldier, without for this reason returning to Christian pacifism, which is only the passive form of sacrifice.

The old figure of heroism, before the great French Revolution, was the figure of the individual warrior. It was the central figure in all the great epic poems of all countries, and continued to support the monarchy and nobility's conception of the lustrous deed, based on personal 'glory'. This figure does not formalise a disciplined relationship to an idea. It is a figure of self-affirmation, the promotion of a visible superiority. It is not a figure of creative freedom, since the classical hero, in the form of the warrior, rather assumes a destiny, or brings to bear an inherited condition. The figure of the warrior is a combination of victory and destiny, of superiority and obedience. The warrior is strong, but he has no real choice concerning the use of his strength. And very often his death is atrocious and devoid of any clear meaning. The figure of the warrior is certainly situated beyond humanity, because it sits between the human animal and the gods. It is not really a creation, but rather a sort of place, resulting from a supraterrestrial whim. It is an aristocratic figure.

The French Revolution replaced the individual and aristocratic figure of the warrior with the democratic and collective figure of the soldier. This created a new imaginary for the relationship between the human and the inhuman. The great notion was the 'mass uprising', the mobilisation of the revolutionary people, regardless of their condition, against the common enemy. The collective dimension of this figure was essential.

The soldier has no proper name. It is a conscious part of a great discipline, under the power of the Idea. Finally, the soldier is anonymous. You know that in Paris, under the Arc de Triomphe, there is a perpetual flame, which celebrates the Unknown Soldier. Indeed, it belongs to the very essence of the symbolic figure of the soldier to be unknown. The fundamental dimension of the figure of the soldier is precisely the dialectical unity between courageous death and immortality, without the slightest reference either to a personal soul or to a God. Such is the democratic notion of glory, which creates something immortal with collective and anonymous courage. We can speak here of an immanent immortality.

Naturally, this is a poetic idea. From romantic poetry we are familiar with the idea of something eternal that lies within the poetical experience of our world, and not in another, sacred world. So we have a lot of poets, from Victor Hugo to Wallace Stevens, by way of Gerard Manley Hopkins and Charles Péguy, who sang the soldier as a glorious and anonymous figure.

This artistic transformation of the figure of the soldier is important, because in fact it is also a political gesture. It is evident that the figure of the soldier has been paradigmatic throughout the revolutionary sequence of politics. To be 'the soldier of the revolution' was a commonly shared conviction. So here, poetry, as often happens, anticipates and clarifies political subjectivity. This is why I will here look for support in poetry.

I have chosen for you just two poems: first, an English one, written by Gerard Manley Hopkins in 1888; and then an American one, written by Wallace Stevens in 1944. What these two poems have in common is the idea of a sort of reciprocity between the heroism of the soldier and a victory over death that is both anonymous and nonreligious – even if Hopkins directly poeticises certain Christian motifs. Here is the poem by Hopkins:

The Soldier

Yes. Why do we all, seeing of a soldier, bless him? bless
Our redcoats, our tars? Both these being, the greater
    part,
But frail clay, nay but foul clay. Here it is: the heart,
Since, proud, it calls the calling manly, gives a guess
That, hopes that, makes believe, the men must be no
    less;
It fancies, feigns, deems, dears the artist after his art;
And fain will find as sterling all as all is smart,
And scarlet wear the spirit of war there express.

Mark Christ our King. He knows war, served this
    soldiering through;
He of all can handle a rope best. There he bides in bliss
Now, and seeing somewhere some man do all that man
    can do,

For love he leans forth, needs his neck must fall on, kiss,
And cry 'O Christ-done deed! So God-made-flesh
    does too:
Were I come o'er again' cries Christ 'it should be this.'[3]

Just three comments:

1. As far as Hopkins is concerned, the question is clearly the question of a figure, a paradigm. Everybody blesses the soldier; everybody blesses the pure appearance of the soldier: 'Our redcoats, our tars'. It is because this appearance is 'the spirit of war'. The soldier belongs to the world of the visible, to immediate, or sensible, symbolic representation. The soldier is the formal visibility of the spirit of war.

2. Why is this 'spirit of war' so important? Because it is the expression of human capacities, beyond risk, beyond death. It is a situation in which the human being is as complete and victorious as God himself was under the name of 'Christ'. Since Christ is the incarnation of God in his salvific function, and thus beyond the simple identity of God, the anonymous soldier, in whom we can see 'some man do all that man can do', is the incarnation of humanity in its becoming, beyond its animal precariousness, beyond its fear-and-trembling

---

3 *Translator's Note*: See Gerard Manley Hopkins, 'The Soldier', *Poems of Gerard Manley Hopkins*, ed. Robert Bridges (London: Humphrey Milford, 1918).

before death. For this reason, just as the true essence of God is achieved in the guise of Christ, so the very essence of humanity is delivered by the figure of the soldier.

3. But this essence of humanity goes beyond a mere accomplishment. It is more existential than essential. The soldier is a figure who transfigures humanity. This is because, in the deed of the soldier, we obtain something eternal – exactly as in the death of Christ, we have the Resurrection, the new life. Witness the cry of God Himself seeing the soldier: 'O Christ-done deed!'

In the end we can say that the soldier is a metaphor that contains three fundamental features of the human being when he or she is seized by a truth: First, it is an example for everybody, a universal address; second, it is the very type of what can be done by somebody when it was thought that nothing was possible – it is the creation of a new possibility; third, it is an example of what is immortal, or eternal, in an action which is at the service of a true idea – it is the creation of an immanent immortality.

We can find all this in Stevens, too, but in a more melancholic fashion. Wallace Stevens is, in my opinion, the greatest American poet of the twentieth century. He was born in 1879, so he was a young man during the First World War. And he died in 1955, so he also knew the horrible massacres of the Second World War. He is a contemporary of the culmination, but also of the end, of the universality of the figure of the soldier. We can see this in the titles of his poems during this period. In 1943 Stevens published a collection under the title *Parts of a World*. As you see, this title incorporates the idea of the end of the world as a perfect totality. In the collection, we find the explicit question of the hero. One great poem in the collection is devoted to the hero in a time of war, the conclusion of which is uncertain with regard to the power or value of the figure of the soldier.[4] However, the poem I have chosen is from his next published collection, *Transport to Summer*. 'Summer' in Stevens is always the name of affirmation, exactly as the sun is the name of the point where being and appearing are indiscernible. For Stevens, war has ceased being the natural site of the new heroism, for war is the end of the evidence of the sun, and of the purely affirmative summer. The question then becomes the following: How, after all those wars in which the human material has been squandered to no end, can a 'transport to summer' still be conceived? Can we hope, once more, after the death of the paradigmatic soldier, for something like the true appearance of being and affirmative thinking? The soldier, for Stevens, is the hero who stands on the threshold of his own necessary sublation by another figure, secretly ciphered in the poem.

The title of the poem is in French: 'Esthétique du Mal'. It is a quotation from Baudelaire. This title tells us that the poem is situated between aesthetics and evil, between the subsistence of figural beauty and its melancholic disappearance.

---

4   *Translator's Note*: See Wallace Stevens, 'Examination of the Hero in a Time of War', in *The Collected Poems of Wallace Stevens*, pp. 273–81.

The figure of the soldier is found in the seventh stanza, which reads as follows:

How red the rose that is the soldier's wound
The wounds of many soldiers, the wounds of all
The soldiers that have fallen, red in blood,
The soldier of time grown deathless in great size.

A mountain in which no ease is ever found,
Unless indifference to deeper death
Is ease, stands in the dark, a shadows' hill
And there the soldier of time has deathless rest.
Concentric circles of shadows, motionless,
Of their own part, yet moving on the wind,
Form mystical convolutions in the sleep
Of time's red soldier deathless on his bed.

The shadows of his fellows ring him round
In the high night, the summer breathes for them
Its fragrance, a heavy somnolence, and for him,
For the soldier of time, it breathes a summer sleep,

In which his wound is good because life was.
No part of him was ever part of death.
A woman smoothes her forehead with her hand
And the soldier of time lies calm beneath that stroke.[5]

---

5   *Translator's Note*: See Wallace Stevens, 'Esthétique du Mal', *The Collected Poems of Wallace Stevens*, pp. 318–19.

Once again, three comments:

1. The soldier is not represented here, as he was in Hopkins, by his external appearance or by his act. He is represented by wounds and death. The colour is the colour of blood. Yet, we find a positive transformation, insofar as it is the rose that formalises the wound ('How red the rose that is the soldier's wound'). And the wound itself, like the rose, is the symbol of the grace of life: 'his wound is good because life was'. So the soldier is an affirmative mediation between life and death.

2. The soldier is composed of time. Every soldier is a 'soldier of time'. Why? Because war – modern war – does not comprise brilliant battles with great warriors who endure a personal destiny. The modern war is a long period of suffering for millions of anonymous soldiers, an obscure period of exposure to death, in the mud and amid the ruins. And yet, this time creates something beyond time; this death creates something beyond death. The whole poem establishes an opaque relationship, which is nevertheless poetically essential, between time and immortality. The formula for this relationship is 'The soldier of time grown deathless in great size'. Here we see the ultimate force of the figure of the soldier at the very moment when he is swallowed up in the barbarism of States. There is in the soldier something great, because in spite of everything, in anonymity, he creates a link without God between time and immortality.

3. And finally, we can say that the soldier is a new form of the evidence of the sun, of the creative power of summer. The summer is present in the night of death: 'In the high night, the summer breathes for them / Its fragrance, a heavy somnolence, and for him, / For the soldier of time, it breathes a summer sleep'. In this sense, touched by the evidence of summer, the dying soldier remains untouched by death: 'No part of him was ever part of death'. That is why the soldier should not at all be confused with the various forms of religious sacrifice, even though his figure is summed up in the mortal body and the bloody wound. Though dead, the soldier remains life itself, the rose, the immortality of the summer in the night.

What can we conclude from all this? The soldier has been the modern symbol of two very important features of the capacity of human animals to create something beyond their own limits, and thus to participate in the creation of a few eternal truths. First, in the figure of the soldier, we know that this creation can be immanent and collective, without depending on religious faith. Second, we know that this creation is eternal within time itself, and not after time.

However, the limit of the figure is made clear in the two poems, as well. With Hopkins, we see that the necessary metaphor of the soldier's figural glory remains within the paradigm of Christianity. The soldier repeats the act of death and resurrection. The human being can be equivalent to a God, says Hopkins. But what happens if God is dead, as

Nietzsche teaches all of us? With Stevens, we have the melancholic survival of summer and sun, expressed by a poetic transfiguration of wounds and death. But what happens if war, in our days, has become one giant obscure slaughter?

The poetic transfiguration of the soldier is also the splendid beginning of the end of this figure. We thus know our task to be a very precise one. The period of the aristocratic warrior is behind us, as is the period of the democratic soldier. So much is certain, but we do not find ourselves for this reason at the peaceful end of History. On the contrary, we live in confusion, violence and injustice. We must create new symbolic forms for our collective actions. We cannot do so in a context of global negation and 'final war', as was the case for much of the twentieth century. We are bound to uphold the new truths in the context of their local affirmation, encircled by endless conflicts. We must find a new sun – in other words, a new mental country. As Stevens says: 'The sun is the country wherever he is'.[6]

---

6   *Translator's Note*: See Stevens, 'Esthétique du Mal', *The Collected Poems of Wallace Stevens*, p. 318.

Chapter Three

Politics as a Nonexpressive Dialectics

I think we can speak today, with regard to the last century, of a classical revolutionary politics. And my thesis is that we are beyond this classical revolutionary politics, whose most important characteristic is what I term its expressive dialectics. Certainly, even in the classical conception, political struggles, insurrections or revolutions are not structural effects – they are moments, and we have to seize the moment, name the circumstances and so on. But the moment, the political struggle, expresses and concentrates social contradictions.[1] This is why an insurrection can be purely singular and at the same time universal: purely singular, because it is a moment, the pure moment; and universal, because finally this moment is the expression of general and fundamental contradictions.

In the same way – this is another aspect of expressive dialectics – the revolutionary party, the revolutionary organisation, represents the working class. Here we come

---

1 *Translator's Note*: An allusion to Lenin's statement to the effect that 'politics is a concentrated expression of economics', which for him represents 'the ABC of Marxism'. See for instance Vladimir I. Lenin, 'Once Again on the Trade Unions, the Current Situation, and the Mistakes of Trotsky and Bukharin', in Lenin, *Collected Works*, vol. 32 (Moscow: Progress Publishers, 1965), p. 83.

back to the famous sentence of Lenin about what constitutes the very heart of Marxism: 'The masses are divided into classes, classes are represented by parties, and parties are led by leaders.'[2] So finally we have something that goes from the historical action of the masses to some proper names. The name of a great leader is the symbolic expression of the totality of the political process in its becoming. Technically, we could say that to go from the moment of creativity of the masses to the true consideration of the contradiction of classes, we have to situate ourselves under the power of proper names such as Leninism, Stalinism, Trotskyism, Castroism or Maoism. And this is also why the question of leadership, the question of the place of proper names in the political field today, is a very important one. Because this conception of masses, classes and proper names – which is at the same time the conception of the relation between singularity and universality, the singularity of the proper name in the face of the absolute universality of the action of the masses – is a very strong one. Alas, this conception is probably saturated, finished. Thus, my goal here is just to try to open the way for a nonexpressive conception of political dialectics, for a conception of political dialectics that forbids this type of passage to the proper name from the action of the masses. In this new conception, revolutionary politics is no longer the expression of the concentration of social

---

2   *Translator's Note*: See Lenin, *'Left-wing' Communism, An Infantile Disorder*, in Lenin, *Selected Works*, vol. 3 (Moscow: Foreign Languages Publishing House, 1961), p. 393.

contradictions; it is a new way of thinking and doing collective action.

In this way, the political process is not the singular expression of objective reality; it is in some sense separated from this reality. It is a process not of expression but of separation. Exactly as in the Platonic vision of dialectics, a truth is separated from opinions; or again, as in the Lacanian conception, where truth is separated from knowledge. It is thus not a contradiction, nor a negation, but a separation.

As you can see, I am really speaking of a politics of truth, because I am speaking about the possibility – the logical and real possibility – of a politics of separation. In the actual field of politics today, which is somehow devastated, a battlefield without armies, we often oppose a reactionary politics – liberalism, say – the crucial concept of which is law and order, which are the protection of power and wealth, to a revolutionary politics, the crucial concept of which is collective desire, the desire for a new world of peace and justice. Now, expressive dialectics today consists in the relation between the conservative dimension of the law and the creative dimension of desire. I would like to show that, in the field of nonexpressive dialectics, a real political truth is situated beyond the opposition between law and desire.

I will begin from a distant point of origin. In fact, I will start with a bit of a logical joke. Suppose you have a bowl usually filled with delicious fruit: apples, pears, strawberries, plums and so on. As you can see, this kind of bowl constitutes the beginning of a real desire! But one day, nobody knows why, the contents of the bowl are completely turned upside down – next to the apples, pears, strawberries or plums, we also find a sinister mixture of stones, snails, pieces of dried mud, dead frogs and thistles. As you see, this is the beginning of a demand for order: the immediate separation of what is tasty from what is disgusting. The problem here is one of classification. So here is the real beginning of my logical joke. What are exactly the correct parts of the contents of this bowl after the metamorphosis in question?

Consider the contents of the bowl as a pure set. The elements of this set, that of the contents of the bowl, are clearly apples, strawberries, thistles, dried mud, dead frogs and so on. No problem. But what are the parts of the bowl – or, if you prefer, the subsets – of this set made up of the contents of the bowl? On one side, we have some parts with a well-defined name. Take for example the part of all the strawberries: it is a part of the bowl, a clear part. You may also choose as a part all the dead frogs. This is a disgusting part, but not for this reason any less a part, a part which bears a well-defined name. You can also have a larger, or more general part: for example, the part made up of all the fruit. It is also a part that has a clear name. We can say that this kind of part is associated in language with a clear predicate. It is, if you want, a predicative part. But, on the other side, you have some very strange multiplicities. What can we say about a part composed of two apples, three thistles and three pieces of dried mud? It is certainly a part of the contents of the bowl. But it is no less certainly a part without a name, without a clearly defined name. You can draw up a list of the elements of this kind of part, or of this kind of subset; you can say there is this, and that, and that. But you cannot have a synthetic name – only an enumeration. Now, generally speaking, a law – what we can name a law – is the prescription of a reasonable order in that sort of situation, when you have that kind of bowl. A law is the decision to accept as really existing only some parts of the bowl of collective life. Of course, the simplest solution is to accept only those parts with a clear name: strawberries, pears, fruits, prickles, mud; and to forbid the parts that have no name at all, such as the mixture of apples, thistles and dead frogs. So the law always determines not only what is permitted and forbidden, but in fact what exists under a clear name, which is normal, and what is unnameable and so does not really exist, which means that it is an abnormal part of the practical totality. It is a very important point to remark, finally, that a law is always a decision about existence.

The problem stems from the fact that a certain part of the collective totality practically does not exist in the framework of the legal conception. The question of the law is finally not only a juridical and classical question but also an ontological one: a question of existence. And, in the last resort, it is a question of the relation of language and things with existence, which is constructed on the basis of the relation between words and things, as Michel Foucault would put it. Finally, in the field of the law there exists only what responds to a clear description. The problem now is on the side of desire, because we can certainly say that desire is always the desire of something which in some sense, with regard to the law, does not exist. Desire is the search for something that is situated beyond the normality of the law. The real object of true desire is always something like an apple that is at the same time a thistle: the desire of a monster. And why? Because desire is the affirmation of pure singularity across and beyond normality.

There is a very simple mathematical example of this relation between desire and law, between different forms of existence. In set theory, we have a theory of pure multiplicity – and suppose we consider one set, no matter what set: a multiplicity that is absolutely any whatsoever. The interesting point is that, by a few technical means, we can formalise the idea of a subset of this set as having a clear name. The question of the relation between existence and a clear name receives a possible formalisation in the framework of mathematical set theory. To be more precise, having a clear name means being defined by a clear formula. This is an invention of the greatest logician of the twentieth century, Kurt Gödel. He named this kind of subset a 'constructible' subset. A constructible subset is a subset of a set that corresponds to a clear description. Ordinarily, we name 'constructible set' a set that is a subset constructible from another set.

So here we are given the possibility of what I would call a great law. A great law is a law of laws or, if you prefer, the law of what is meant by the possibility of a law. And we have a sort of mathematical example of this type of law, which means a law that bears not only on things or subjects, but on laws themselves. The great law takes the form of a very simple axiom, the name of which is the 'axiom of constructibility', which holds that all sets are constructible. This is a decision about existence: you decide that the only sets to exist are constructible and you have, as a simple formula, a simple decision about existence. All sets are constructible: such is the law of laws. And this is a genuine possibility. You can decide that all sets are constructible. Why? Because all mathematical theorems that can be demonstrated in the general framework of set theory can also be demonstrated with regard to constructible sets. Therefore, everything that is true in the universe of sets in general is true for the universe composed solely of constructible sets. So – and this is very important for the general question of the law – we are capable of deciding that all sets are constructible or that every multiplicity is governed by the law; and, in so doing, we lose nothing: all that is true in general is also true with the restriction to constructible sets. If we lose nothing, if the field of truth is the same under the axiom of constructibility, then we can conclude something like the following: the law is not a restriction of life and thinking; in the framework of the law, the liberty of living and thinking is the same. The mathematical model of that is that we lose nothing when we affirm that all sets are constructible; that is to say, all parts of a set are constructible, or, finally, all parts have a clear definition. We thus obtain a general classification of parts, a rational classification – and somehow a classification of society – without any loss of truth.

At this point it is important to note a very interesting fact, a pure fact, which is that practically no mathematician admits the axiom of constructibility. It is a splendid order, a splendid world: all in it is constructible. But this splendid order does not stimulate the desire of the mathematicians, as conservative as they may be. And why? Because the desire of the mathematician is to go beyond the clear order of nomination and constructibility. The desire of the mathematician is the desire for a mathematical monster. They certainly want a law – it is difficult to do mathematics without laws – but the desire to find a new mathematical monster is situated beyond this law.

On this point modern mathematics rejoins classical theology. You probably know the famous text of Saint Paul in Romans 7. The direct correlation between law and desire appears here under the name of sin: 'If it had not been for the law, I should not have known sin. I should not have known what it is to covet if the law had not said you shall not covet.' Sin is that dimension of desire that finds its object beyond and after the prescription by the law. Finally, this means finding the object that is without name.

The mathematical example is very striking here. After Gödel, after the definition of constructible sets and the refusal of the axiom of constructibility by the majority of mathematicians, the question of the mathematician's desire has become: How can we find a nonconstructible set? You immediately see the difficulty, which is of great political consequence. The difficulty is: How can we find a mathematical object without a clear description, without name, without place in the classification? How to find an object the characteristic of which is to have no name, to not be constructible? In the 1960s Paul Cohen found a complex and elegant solution for naming or identifying a set which is not

constructible, which has no name, no place in the great classification of predicates – a set without a specific predicate.
It was a great victory of desire against the law, in the field
of law itself – the field of mathematics. And as with many
things, many victories of this kind, this happened in the
1960s. Cohen gives the nonconstructible sets a magnificent
name: 'generic' sets. And this invention takes place amid the
revolutionary actions of the sixties.

You know that Marx gives the name 'generic humanity' to
humanity in the movement of its self-emancipation, and that
'proletariat' – the name 'proletariat' – is the name of the possibility of generic humanity in its affirmative form. 'Generic',
for Marx, names the becoming of the universality of human
being, and the historical function of the proletariat is to
deliver us this generic form of the human being. So in Marx
the political truth is situated on the side of genericity, and
never on the side of particularity. Formally, it is a question of
desire, creation or invention, and not a matter of law, necessity or conservation. So for Cohen – as well as for Marx – the
pure universality of multiplicity, of sets, is not to be sought on
the side of correct definition or clear description but on the
side of nonconstructibility. The truth of sets is generic.

Let us now talk about the consequences of all this at the
level of politics. The field of politics always presents itself
in concrete situations as the dialectical field of law and
constructibility, on the one hand, and of desire and genericity, on the other. But this is by no means a political division.
Nowhere are there people who would declare themselves
in favour of desire against people who would be in favour

of the law. The political struggle is not directly the struggle between genericity and constructibility. Such a view is purely formal. In fact, we have complex compositions that mix law, order, desire, genericity, constructibility. Fascism, for example, is not entirely on the side of law. As empirical studies show, fascism is the total destruction of law in favour of a special conception of desire for an entirely particular object. This object, which is national, racial and so on, is neither constructible nor generic. It is only the negation of certain other objects, the destruction of these others. Finally, there exists in fascism the mythic desire for an object the true essence of which is death. And the real of fascism is something like a law of death, which is the result of a particular composition of genericity and constructibility.

Significantly, in the classical conception, revolutionary vision is not at all situated on the side of pure desire, because the contents of revolutionary desire are the realisation of generic humanity, which in fact represents the end of the separate relation between law and desire. In this case, the goal is something like the fusion of law and desire, so as to arrive at something that would be like the creative affirmation of humanity as such. We could say that this kind of vision presents a law of life. Thus, the classical contradiction between fascism and the revolutionary conception presents us with two different compositions of genericity and constructibility, with the law of death on one side and the law of life on the other side.

To describe our current situation, we should invoke two great paradigms of the dialectical relation between law and desire. The first paradigm is the idea of the unity of law and desire, by the strict limitation of the legality of desire as such, by the delimitation of correct desire. This corresponds in fact to the axiom of constructibility. We find ourselves today under the rule of the axiom of constructibility – that is to say, the restriction of existing desires to the clear nomination of normal desires. The reactionary conception is the reactionary conception of desire itself; it is not at all the pure opposition – the oppressive opposition – between law and desire. The key concept is not that of law against desire. It is on the contrary the dictatorship of normal desires – with a very open conception of the normal, to be sure, but not as wide as we sometimes imagine. You can suppose, for example, that representative democracy is the normal desire of all the people in the world. This is, strictly speaking, a constructible conception of political desire: only one type of political figure is admitted as a constructible subset of all political possibilities. And then you can embark upon a terrible war to impose this form of the State all across the world. As you can observe, this has nothing to do with the law. In fact, this provokes great disorder. In Iraq, it is not a question of law and order; it is a question of blood and total disorder. But it is a constructible choice, the goal being to impose everywhere the construction of a political name that is supposed to be completely clear.

This is the first position. The second is the idea of desire as a search beyond the law for something illegal but generic. It is the idea that political universality is always the development of a new conception, a new composition of social reality – that is, if you want, the complete transformation of the contents of the bowl. This new composition is really the objective of political change between blacks and whites, men and women, different nationalities, rich and poor, and so on. All of this can be effectuated beyond clearly defined names and separations. It is a practical process, a political process that creates something generic. So in the second conception a political process is always the local creation of something generic. As for Cohen, the point is to find or create a part of the totality of life that is generic. In this case, there is always something like a dictatorship, which is what Rousseau called the despotism of liberty, but which these days is rather the despotism of equality. Against the idea of normal desires we must sustain the militant idea of a desire that permanently affirms the existence of that which has no name. To the extent that it is the common part of our historical existence, we must affirm the existence of that which has no name as the generic part of this historical existence: that is probably the revolutionary conception of our time, with the possibility that this kind of transformation would be local and not necessarily general or total. So it is not at all desire against the law. I completely agree with Slavoj Žižek when he argues that the question of the general will is today the central question of politics. I would only propose to change the adjective, opposing to normal desires not the general will but the generic will.

Thus, my conclusion will not be entirely political. As so often when I find myself in the field of pure possibility, my conclusion is poetic, and I will call upon the great American poet Wallace Stevens. Simon Critchley has recently published a beautiful book about Wallace Stevens, the title of which is *Things Merely Are*. This is a typically poetic affirmation, not a political one. For in the political world, things never 'merely are' what they are – not at all. In one of the poems of Wallace Stevens we can find this sentence: 'The final belief must be in a fiction.'[3] And in fact I believe that the most difficult problem of our time is the problem of a new fiction. We must distinguish between fiction and ideology. Because, generally speaking, ideology is opposed to science, to truth or to reality. But, as we have known since Lacan, truth itself is in a structure of fiction. The process of truth is also the process of a new fiction. Thus, finding the new great fiction offers the possibility of having a final political belief.

And in fact, when the world is sombre and confused, as it is today, we must sustain our final belief by a symbolic fiction. The problem of young people in poor neighbourhoods or *cités* is the problem of the absence of a fiction. It has nothing to do with a social problem. The problem is the lack of a great fiction as support for a great belief. Thus, the final belief in generic truths, the final possibility of opposing the generic will to normal desires, this type of possibility and the belief in this sort of possibility, in generic truths,

---

3   *Translator's Note*: Stevens writes: 'The prologues are over. It is a question, now, / Of final belief. So, say that final belief / Must be in a fiction. It is time to choose', in 'Asides on the Oboe', *The Collected Poems of Wallace Stevens*, p. 250. Compare Simon Critchley, *Things Merely Are: Philosophy in the Poetry of Wallace Stevens* (New York: Routledge, 2005).

has to be our new fiction. No doubt the difficulty lies in the fact that we must find a great fiction without possessing a proper name for it. This is my conviction, even if I cannot really demonstrate this point here. In the last century, all the great fictional dispositions of the political field had their proper names. For me the problem today is not to renounce fiction – because without great fiction we can have no great belief and no great politics – but probably to have a fiction without a proper name. The point is to find another disposition between masses, classes, parties; another composition of the political field, because a great fiction is always something like the name of a recomposition of the political field itself. The great fiction of communism, which goes from masses to proper names through the mediation of class struggles, is the form of the classical revolutionary recomposition of the political field. And so we have to find a new fiction, to find our final belief in a local possibility for finding something generic.

In the same collection, Wallace Stevens – speaking about fiction, about the final belief that is a fiction – also writes: 'It is possible, possible, possible. It must be possible.'[4] Such is indeed our problem today. It must be possible. At issue no doubt is a new form of courage. We most certainly have to create the real possibility of our fiction, which is a generic fiction under a new form. The new localisation no doubt poses the question of a new political courage. To find the

---

4   *Translator's Note*: See Wallace Stevens, 'Notes toward a Supreme Fiction', *The Collected Poems of Wallace Stevens*, p. 404.

fiction is a question of justice and hope. But the question of the real possibility of a fiction is a question of courage. Courage is the name of something that cannot be reduced to either law or desire. It is the name of subjectivity irreducible to the dialectics of law and desire in its ordinary form. Now, today, the place of political action – not that of political theory, political conceptions or representations, but political action as such – is precisely something irreducible to either law or desire, which creates the place, the local place, for something like the generic will. And, about this place, let us say, like Stevens: it is possible, possible, possible, it must be possible. Perhaps. We hope, we must hope that it will be possible to find the possibility of our new fiction.

Sources

'The Enigmatic Relationship between Philosophy and Politics' is the transcription of a talk originally presented in French as the closing plenary of the *Journées Alain Badiou,* which took place in Paris on 22–24 October 2010, at the École Normale Supérieure (rue d'Ulm) and the Campus des Cordeliers.

'The Figure of the Soldier' was first presented as a talk in English at the University of California in Los Angeles, in May 2006. The talk, a slightly different version of which also appears online at lacan.com, was translated back into French by Isabelle Vodoz. The present version has been retranslated into English based on Isabelle Vodoz's careful French text authorised by Badiou.

'Politics as a Nonexpressive Dialectics' was first presented as a talk in English, on 26 November 2005, at the Birkbeck Institute for the Humanities, University of London. The transcription by Robin Mackay also appeared as a small pamphlet published by Urbanomic in London. Like the previous talk, this one was translated back into French by Isabelle Vodoz, and for the present publication has been rendered into English based on the published French text.

Appendix: Reflections on the Crisis in Quebec

François Gauvin: What do you think of the student conflict in Quebec?

Alain Badiou: What I find interesting first of all is the scale and determination of the phenomenon. Basically, what is happening in your country is a sudden and widespread resistance to a global phenomenon, which is trying to apply the business model to every kind of human activity. Like a business, the university is supposed to become self-financing, whereas historically it was built up according to quite different rules. The conflict obviously took the particular and very localised form of a fight against the planned rise in university fees, which then spread to an opposition to the government's handling of the crisis. But it is clear that at the core of the uprising is a subjectivity in revolt against the idea that business should be the paradigm for everything. And this point of resistance is now mobilising a large-scale debate which concerns us all, and the outcome of which is not predictable.

F.G.: Would you make a comparison with the student revolt of May 1968, when you were a Maoist leader calling for revolution?

A.B.: Yes, in terms of its ways of acting, its style, its inventiveness. That is the first reminder of May 68, the first great echo of an active, joyful subjectivity that does not shy away from conflict when this is needed. Even if it is dividing Quebec society. It was just the same in 1968. The students attracted sympathy, but as we saw in the June 1968 legislative elections, which were won by the party of General de Gaulle, French society was completely divided.

F.G.: Your involvement with Quebec goes back to that time.

A.B.: Yes. Very soon after May 1968, I went to Montreal as a human rights observer for the trial of Pierre Vallières and Charles Gagnon of the Front de libération du Québec (FLQ). That was my first real contact, my first immersion in Quebec's singular society, which made a strong impression on me.

F.G.: Subsequently, you devoted a whole chapter of your masterwork, Logics of Worlds, *to Quebec. Did Quebec act as a stimulant for your conception of the world?*

A.B.: In the book's overall argument, I took Quebec first of all as a particular example. But you're right to speak of a stimulant. The history of Quebec sums up several features of world history in recent centuries: a long-standing European colonisation, the exceptional presence of two world powers, the English and the French, etcetera. There is no equivalent to this anywhere else. And that created a society, a subjectivity, which combined terms that are not normally combined. So it really is, for me, what I call a 'world'. The history of

Quebec is marked by phenomena that are at the same time irreducibly particular and yet have an innovatory universal character. That is still the case today. I would say: Always keep an eye on Quebec.

F.G.: You say that Quebec is a world in the process of becoming ['devenir-monde']. But what does a world mean for you?

A.B.: In a very general sense, a world is a regime of relations of identities and differences. In order to say what is particular about this world, to simplify, if you take a human world there have to be identities – national, linguistic, the common consciousness of belonging to this world, etcetera – and differences. In the case of Quebec, of course, the French language is an element of identity, but it is so necessarily in relation to the omnipresent Anglophony and the fact that there have been, and still are, Amerindians who do not immediately have this identity, and so on. From this point of view, Quebec has an absolutely singular history. I speak of it as a world in the making [*faire-monde*] that is still open, as I'm not sure Quebec really has resolved the problem of the world that it is in the process of becoming. The present episode of revolt is part of this, of the Quebecers making-world, and its interest for everyone.

F.G.: But isn't every society a world in the making? France, for example.

A.B.: Identities here are more rigid. It's a country in latent crisis, a former planetary great power, with a particular universality, which does not know what to do with its lost greatness. From this point of view, France is at least as much a world being unmade as a world being made. My proposition is that we have to put an end to France.

F.G.: Pardon?

A.B.: I've thought for a long time that France should merge with Germany. I'm very happy, moreover, that other people, such as Michel Serres, now share my opinion. There is no future for France alone. The European combination is teetering, as we've seen with Greece, and everyone understands that France and Germany form the hard core of Europe. A merger would make it possible to stand up to the other economic great powers, which neither France nor Germany – nor Europe – is capable of doing today. The French and German economies are already intertwined, so let's have this hard core realised politically! That could be in the form of a federal State, as is already the case with Germany.

F.G.: And with Canada . . . But the independentists hope that the demonstrations of solidarity aroused by the crises will help their cause. Is this the start of a new history?

A.B.: I certainly don't know enough about the internal situation of Quebec to say so. But I have a certain distrust of the independentists. In the last twenty or thirty years, we have witnessed the break-up of national entities, sometimes their fragmentation: Yugoslavia, Czechoslovakia, Somalia, Congo . . . You have to be very vigilant as to the real meaning of state disintegrations. They are negative phenomena of contemporary history, often responsible for tragic human situations. Well, you're going to say: 'But Quebec isn't like that!'

F.G.: You're taking the words out of my mouth . . .

A.B.: I don't spontaneously support a secession by Quebec, without really powerful arguments. I am not sure the path of the Quebec world in the making absolutely needs a state separatism. I believe it is possible to negotiate consistent federalisms, and that this is a better formula.

Suggested Further Reading

Texts by Alain Badiou

ON THE LINK BETWEEN POLITICS AND PHILOSOPHY IN GENERAL

'Philosophy and Politics', in Alain Badiou, *Conditions*, translated by Steve Corcoran (London: Continuum, 2008), pp. 147–76

'Philosophy and Politics', in Alain Badiou, *Infinite Thought: Truth and the Return of Philosophy*, translated and edited by Oliver Feltham and Justin Clemens (London: Continuum, 2005), pp. 69–78

Metapolitics, translated by Jason Barker (London: Verso, 2005)

Badiou argues against the tradition of political philosophy, which he associates with the likes of Hannah Arendt and Claude Lefort, by proposing to think not of 'the political' (*le politique*) but of 'politics' (*la politique*) as an active form of thinking, or thought-practice, in its own right. He then goes on to evaluate the proximity of this proposal for a 'metapolitical' orientation to the work of his teacher Louis Althusser and his contemporaries Jacques Rancière and Sylvain Lazarus, before offering case studies on the concepts of democracy, justice and Thermidoreanism.

ON THE CONTINUED PROMISES AND
LIMITS OF TRADITIONAL MARXISM

Can Politics Be Thought? and *Of an Obscure Disaster: On the End of the Truth of the State*, translated by Bruno Bosteels (Durham, NC: Duke University Press, forthcoming)

In *Can Politics Be Thought?* (originally published in 1985) Badiou offers a two-pronged reassessment – both destruction and recomposition – of the place of Marxism in contemporary political thinking. Marxism today has lost its power as a discursive referent historically tied to the workers' movement, the formation of socialist States and the wars of national liberation. But we can be the subjects rather than the reactive objects of this crisis of Marxism. The fact that 'the political' is in retreat offers a chance for a reopening of politics. *Can Politics Be Thought?* should be read alongside Derrida's *The Politics of Friendship*, Rancière's *Disagreement* and Lyotard's *Enthusiasm*, all of which were first presented as part of a seminar on 'the political' organised by Philippe Lacoue-Labarthe and Jean-Luc Nancy at the École Normale Supérieure in rue d'Ulm. *Of an Obscure Disaster* is Badiou's take on the collapse of the Soviet Union and the so-called death of communism.

'Evental Sites and Historical Situations', in Alain Badiou, *Being and Event*, translated by Oliver Feltham (London: Continuum, 2005), pp. 173–7

'The Factory as Event Site', translated by Alberto Toscano and Nina Power, *Prelom* 8 (1991), pp. 171–6

'Thirty Ways of Easily Recognising an Old-Marxist', translated by Alberto Toscano and Nina Power, *Prelom* 8 (1991), pp. 177–9

ON THE LESSONS OF HISTORY FOR POLITICS

'Historicity of Politics: Lessons of Two Revolutions', in Alain Badiou, *Polemics*, translated by Steve Corcoran (London: Verso, 2006), pp. 257–328

The Rebirth of History: Times of Riots and Uprisings, translated by Gregory Elliott (London: Verso, 2012)

The Rebirth of History is Badiou's take on the Arab Spring and, to a lesser extent, the Spanish *indignados* and the various Occupy movements in the US. After a brief and in many ways quite traditional analysis of the difference between riots as short-lived insurrections, movements as historical moments, and the need for properly political organisation, Badiou goes on to tie in the contemporary scene of politics with his own philosophical project in the wake of *Logics of Worlds*.

ON THE PLACE OF MAOISM WITH
RESPECT TO MARXISM–LENINISM

Theory of the Subject, translated by Bruno Bosteels
(London: Continuum, 2009)

This early summary of Badiou's thought (originally published
in 1982) is written in the name of 'we Marxists' or 'we hand-
ful of Maoists'. It proposes a thorough recasting of the
Hegelian dialectic as a logic of scission or splitting, attuned
to the Maoist maxim: 'One divides into two.' Published at
the time of Mitterrand's arrival in the presidential office, the
book went completely against the grain of the consensus of
its time and received little or no attention either in the main-
stream press or among militant philosophers.

Les années rouges (Paris: Les Prairies Ordinaires, 2012)

A re-edition of Badiou's three Maoist books from the
1970s: *Theory of Contradiction*, *Of Ideology* and *The
Rational Kernel of the Hegelian Dialectic*, with a new preface
written especially for the French edition. A didactic over-
view of Maoism, as well as scathing attacks on Althusser,
the philosophers of desire Deleuze–Guattari and Lyotard,
and the 'New Philosopher' André Glucksmann.

ON THE FIGURE OF THE MILITANT WITHOUT A PARTY

Saint Paul: The Foundation of Universalism, translated by
Ray Brassier (Stanford: Stanford University Press, 2003)

Badiou reads Paul's letters as the formal model of militant fidelity without a party. Paul is to Christ what Lenin is to Marx. At the same time, however, Paul is an antiphilosopher and, therefore, many of the more dogmatic or absolutist ('ultraleftist' or 'Marcionist') elements in Paul's attitude toward the event should not be associated with Badiou's own position. The book on Paul is part of a four-year-long investigation into the seductive powers and limitations of the antiphilosophical tradition, which also includes studies of Nietzsche, Wittgenstein and Lacan.

ON THE RENEWAL OF COMMUNISM

'The Idea of Communism', in Costas Douzinas and Slavoj Žižek, eds, *The Idea of Communism* (London: Verso, 2010), pp. 1–14

The Communist Hypothesis, translated by David Macey and Steve Corcoran (London: Verso, 2010)

Badiou proposes to historicise the communist Idea according to three sequences, the third of which might currently be opening. As opposed to the previous two sequences, from 1792 until 1871 (dominated by the question of communism's existence), and from 1917 until 1976 (dominated by the question of communism's victory and state-sponsored imposition), the task of the third sequence would be to find ways of reaffirming the sheer existence of the communist hypothesis in an age that has seen the last revolution take place in the Chinese Cultural Revolution. Thus, we are closer to the situation faced by Marx and Engels in the 1840s than to the past century's state-oriented politics of most communist parties.

Secondary Literature

ON BADIOU AND POLITICS

Bruno Bosteels, *Badiou and Politics* (Durham, NC: Duke University Press, 2011)

Against the supposition of a break between the early, dialectical Badiou and the later, mathematical writings since *Being and Event*, this books argues for a dialectical reading of all of Badiou's work. The chapter 'One Divides into Two' discusses the activities of Badiou's militant organisation UCFML (Union des Communistes de France Marxiste-Léniniste) in the 1970s and their theoretical repercussions for questions pertaining to the link between politics and philosophy in the guise of post-Maoism.

Peter Hallward, 'Politics: Equality and Justice', *Badiou: A Subject to Truth* (Minneapolis: University of Minnesota Press, 2003), pp. 223–42

Still the most complete introduction to Badiou's overall philosophical system. Hallward faults Badiou for being absolutist and paying but scant attention to matters of historical mediation and relationality. The chapter on politics offers a detailed account of the achievements and shortcomings of Badiou's group Organisation Politique in the late 1980s and early 1990s.

ON BADIOU AND MARXISM

Alberto Toscano, 'Marxism Expatriated: Alain Badiou's Turn', in Jacques Bidet and Stathis Kouvelakis, eds, *Critical Companion to Contemporary Marxism* (Leiden: Brill, 2006), pp. 529–48

Toscano focuses on the shift, or turn, in Badiou's thinking about politics and Marxism that occurs on the pages of *Can Politics Be Thought?* From the dominance of a politics of destruction and purification, still sutured onto Maoism, there gradually develops a politics of subtraction that is no longer transitive to history but strictly immanent to its own rationality.

ON BADIOU AND MAOISM

Jason Barker, 'Maoist Beginnings', *Alain Badiou* (London: Pluto Press, 2002)

A useful summary of Badiou's early texts as an Althusserian and his Maoist booklets *Theory of Contradiction* and *Of Ideology*.

Badiou and Cultural Revolution, a special issue of *positions: east asia cultures critique* 13.3 (2005)

Aside from containing an early translation of Badiou's talk on the Chinese Cultural Revolution, this special issue also includes a complete bibliography and selected texts from Badiou's organisation UCFML, as well as an interpretation by the Italian sociologist Alessandro Russo about the last meeting of the Red Guards with Chairman Mao.

ON BADIOU AND CONTEMPORARY POLITICAL THEORY

Antonio Calcagno, *Badiou and Derrida: Politics, Events and Their Time* (London: Continuum, 2007)

Adrian Johnston, *Badiou, Žižek, and Political Transformation: The Cadence of Change* (Evanston: Northwestern University Press, 2009)

Nick Hewlett, *Badiou, Balibar, Rancière: Rethinking Emancipation* (London: Continuum, 2007)

Adam Miller, *Badiou, Marion and St Paul: Immanent Grace* (London: Continuum, 2008)

Printed in the United States
by Baker & Taylor Publisher Services